Bangladeshi Immigrants in Meghalaya

Bangladeshi Immigrants in Meghalaya

Causes of Human Movement and Impact on Garo Hills

Sengjrang N. Sangma

Maulana Abul Kalam Azad Institute of Asian Studies, Kolkata

ANSHAH Anshah Publishing House

ISBN: 81-8364-000-1

First Published in India in 2005

Bangladeshi Immigrants in Meghalaya

Published by:
ANSHAH PUBLISHING HOUSE
H4-03, Mayurdhwaj, 60 I P Extention
Delhi-110092, INDIA
Phone: 9213355060, 9213387134

Preface

The study takes up unauthorized human movement into Garo Hills, Meghalaya during 1964 and in 1971, the periods of political upheaval in earstwhile East Pakistan and the impact of Bangladeshi immigrants on the Garo Hills of Meghalaya.

I am thankful to Maulana Abul Kalam Azad Institute of Asian Studies, Kolkata for the support and cooperation extended for this study.

Sengjrang N. Sangma

Contents

PREFACE 5

INTRODUCTION 9

Chapter I
The Land and the People 11

Chapter II
Relief Operations 19

Chapter III
Cross Border Movement—Causes 40

Chapter IV
The Rehabilitation and Reclamation 64

Chapter V
The Impacts of the Cross Border Movement 87

APPENDIX I 104

APPENDIX II 108

APPENDIX III 109

APPENDIX IV 110

BIBLIOGRAPHY 111

INDEX 115

Introduction

The study of human movement from Bangladesh to Garo Hills of Meghalaya has been taken up because since the period around Independence involving the creation of India, East Pakistan and West Pakistan out of the single sub-continent, the flight of refugees into Garo hills is a frequent occurrence. So frequent is the problem of disturbances along the Indo-Bangladesh border and so great is the problem posed by a huge number of refugees crossing the border at regular intervals since 1947 that the government of India, during the tenure of Mrs. Indira Gandhi as the Prime Minister of India, was compelled to take the extreme step of 'liberating' East Pakistan in 1971. December 16, 1971 is observed by Bangladesh as the day of victory from the rule of West Pakistan.

The problem of unauthorized human movement into India from Bangladesh has had an adverse impact on demographic balance, economy, environment, administrative machinery, social and political condition in India.

The population in the former East Pakistan has the same composite structure as India. Religion wise there are Hindus, Muslims, Christians and those practicing indigenous faiths. On both sides of the border there are Garos, Hajongs, Banias and other scheduled castes. The pattern of flight has been more or lèss the same on every occasion.

This study takes up the human movement into Garo Hills during 1964 and in 1971. Both were periods of political upheaval in East Pakistan/Bangladesh.

The official records of Garo hills show that in 1964 there were no Muslim refugees at all. Greater percentages of refugees were Garos and Hajongs. Classification has been done community wise.

The break up of refugees in 1971 was done according to the breakup of religions groups in official records. The records show that the number of Muslim refugees exceeded Christian refugees. The causes of the flight are also recorded in the available documents.

The shifting of the refugees to interior camps, the management of the camps, the attitude of the government towards them, rehabilitation, land reclamation and repatriation are the subject of study in this research project.

Chapter I

The Land and the People

Garo Hills was a part of Assam state till April, 1970 before Meghalaya was born. On 2nd April, 1970, it was inaugurated as an autonomous state, but full fledged statehood was declared by the Indian Union on January 21, 1972. After the declaration as a State by the Indian Union, it became part of Meghalaya state. Garo Hills was only a small district with head quarters at Tura till 1976. The total area of the district is 8,167 sq. km. It is divided into three district of East, West and South Garo Hills, with head quarters at Williamnagar, Tura and Baghmara respectively. According to 2001 census, the total population of East Garo Hills is 247,555; West Garo Hills 515,813 persons and South Garo Hills 99,105 persons.[2] East Garo Hills district was created in October, 1976 and South Garo Hills district created in June, 1992. There are three sub-divisions: they are Resubelpara subdivision, Dadengre sub-division and Ampati sub-division.

The three district of Garo Hills are situated between 25°9' and 26° of North Latitude and between 89°49' and 91°2' East Longitude.[3] These three districts are bounded on the North and West by the district of Goalpara, Assam and on the South by the district of Mymensing of Bangladesh and on the East by the district of West Khasi Hills of Meghalaya.

Three districts of Garo Hills have two physical divisions, the hills and the plains. The hills of these districts, gradually sloping towards the West. Tura range and Arbella range run parallel to each another, from East to West. The hills of these districts are: Tura, Nokrek, Arbefla, Ranggira, Chitmang and Balpakram. Nokrek is the highest peak in Garo Hills with an altitude of 1,412 meters.

The Tura range and Arbella range of Garo Hills form watersheds, and from these watersheds the rivers flow down towards the plains of Bangladesh in the south and the Brahmaputra valley in the north. A number of rivers which cut the plateau are Dudhnai, Krishnai, Didak, Didram and Jinjiram flowing to the north, Ringge or Rongai and Ganol flowing to the West. Bhogai, Dareng and Simsang flowing towards South into the Surmah valley. Among the rivers of Garo Hills, the Simsang is the longest and is navigable for a distance of about 30 km.[4] It started from Nokrek hills of West Garo Hills, flowing towards East through East Garo Hills and then it turns towards South through the district of south Garo Hills of Meghalaya, into the valley of Sunnah, Bangladesh. The Rongai Valley Project is being constructed for the purpose of irrigation on the Ringge River of the West Garo Hills.

The entire district of Garo Hills is densely wooded. However, due to the practice of slash-and-bum agriculture methods[5] or *'jhum'* by the Garo people, virgin forests and ancient trees have almost disappeared[6] Moreover, this situation is aggravated by the influx of Bangladesh refugees as they are selling trees, bamboos and firewood for their livelihood. Besides trees, there are many rare types of plants such as orchids and pitcher plants.[7]

The People

According to the Pores Garos migrated from Tibet and passed the Himalaya through the low ranges and settled down in Cooch Behar about four hundred years ago. They were led by Jappa, Jalimpa, Suukpa and Bonggipa, whom they referred to as rajas. From Cooch Behar they came to Dhubri and then moved on to Jogigopa, near banks of the Manas tributary. There the local chief wanted the beautiful Garo girl Juge Silche[8] for his wife but the community refused to surrender her. They hid her in a cave near the Bramahputra. Later they were compelled to leave that place. To cross the Bramahputra river they exchanged one Garo girl Dimri for three hundred plantain stems.[9]

With rafts of plantain stems they crossed the Brahmaputra River towards the South. Then they wandered towards Gauhati but they were ill-treated by the ruler. They retraced their steps and settled down near Boko in Kamrup district. In this place there were many "Tiger-men",[10] who oppressed them. Therefore, they moved on to the Habraghat Pargana, which is the present Goalpara district of Assam.[11] For some reason at this point the migrants broke into different branches. Some of them wandered off and entered Garo Hills. In one of the groups was Abong Noga and his wife Silme Doka, who led their people and settled down in Nokrek peak.[12]

Linguistically, Garos belong to one of the Bodo speaking groups and Bodo speaking groups are from the great Tibeto-Burman race. This race was said to have formed in the North-Eastern part of China between the upper waters of Yang-Tse-Kiang and Hwang-Ho believed to have migrated to the head waters of the Irrawady and the Chindwin. Some of them followed the course of the Brahmaputra River and some of them went northwards of Himalaya Mountain and settled down in Tibet. Some sections of them crossed the mountains and spread over the Brahmaputra valley. They settled down along the southern range of the Himalayas from Assam in the East and Punjab in the West. It was believed that in course of time the Tibeto-Burman race occupied the whole of North East India, except Khasi and Jainti Hills, which Mon-Khmer speaking family had already occupied.[13] They had settled down in the Brahmaputra valley, notably in Goalpara and Kamrup District, and Bangladesh. Some of them migrated to the hills along the river valleys. They were head hunters who made numerous raids into the surrounding plain areas. "In 1807, four times within a few days the Garos rushed from their hills, plundered two official head quarters, fired several hamlets, and left the headless corpses of twenty seven men and women on the ground.[14] The Garos believe that the souls of the dead go to a place known to them as Balpakram (the land of the spirits), and that spirit requires the soul of another to attend and carry the things which are given to the dead at the time of death. Hence to send things to the spirit of the dead they were urged to send raiding parties to the plains for head-hunting. They hung up human skulls as trophies in the front verandas of their houses. This continued until the British occupation finally put an end to the practice. In 1873, order was given by Captain Williamson, first Deputy Commissioner of Tura, to bring such trophies and burn them.[15]

Short History

In 1765, Dewani of Bengal came under the British. The British government appointed many tributary chiefs or Zamindars to collect the tribute. Surrounding plain areas of Garo Hills were made under the authority of the Zamindars, who further sought to extend their jurisdiction into the hills. The independent Garos gave fierce resistance, as a result of which, on the out skirts of Garo Hills were seen a series of bloodshed, murder, and raids. Moreover, constant conflicts between the Garos and the Zamindars were due to the extortions made at the weekly markets.[16]

The British government took steps to put an end to these conflicts by appointing a Garo named Rengta as a Zamindar under the company rule in 1790, but the opposition of the Karaibari Zamindar to this more rendered it as a futile move.[17]

The British government sent David Scott, as a Special Commissioner in 1816, to settle the conflicts between the Garos and the Zaminders, this more, however, did not completely succeed in establishing peace. By the new regulation, Garos were exempted from paying tribute to the Zamindar, yet the latter continued to oppress them as before. So the Garos resented the Zamindars and continued to be turbulent.[18]

During 1850s numerous raids were conducted by the Garos on the plain areas of the Goalpara side and in Mymensing district. Therefore, in 1866, decision was taken to depute Lt. W.J. Wiffiamson as Assistant Commissioner to the hills. The action succeeded in bringing that half of the district under British, but the interior villages in the heart of the Garo Hills *were* entirely independent. In 1872, the British Government was compelled to take the extreme measure and occupied the whole Garo Hills.[19] At the end of the year 1872 three expeditions were conducted.[20]

That time, Capt. Dally reached the appointed place which was first among the three groups. The Garo warriors named Togan Nengminja from Samanda village fought them bravely along with his people on the 12th December 1872, at Chisobibra[21] (near the confluence place of Chiso rivulet with Simsang river), but unfortunately he was shot dead on the spot. By this act British could bring the Garos into complete submission.

The Garos live not only on Garo Hills but also in Assam and in the Mymensing district of the present day Bangladesh. According to 1891 census there were around 18,600 Garos in Mymensing district.[22]

In the former days, the Garo spoke different dialects as they lived in different dialectic groups in various parts of the Garo Hills. The different dialects among the Garos are; the A-we, Chisak, Dual, Matchi, Matjangchi, A-beng or Am-beng, Chibok, Ruga Gara or Ganching, Atong and

Me-gam. Among these some dialects like Ruga are almost disappearing. It is due to the British occupation of the district, where they called upon the Missionaries to introduce Christian Religion in schools. The American Baptist missionaries were the first to came to Garo Hills and they learned the A-we dialect to write text books and translated the Bible and made it the standard literature in Garo language.

Though the Garos called themselves, 'A-chik' or 'Mande', but no one could really prove the etymological meaning of the 'Garo'.

The Garo society maintains a matrilineal system. They take their title from the side of the mother and not from the father. Heiress always inherits the family property, it never goes to a son. There are five main clans among the Garos: Sangma, Marak, Momin, Arengh and Shira. These clans are divided into many sub-clans. Original inhabitants of the district, the Garos, used to write their main clan against their names, but the Garos migrating from the Bangladesh used to write their sub-clan.

In Garo Hills although Garo constitute majority inhabitants of the district in the hills, yet many other minority communities have drifted into surrounding plain areas of the district.

They are: Rabhas, Hajongs, Koches, Rajbongsis, Mech and the Bodo-Kacharies.[24]

References

1. Marak, C.R., *Influence of English on Garo Poetry*, New Delhi, Scholar Publishing House (P) Ltd. 1985. p. 10.

2. Provisional Census Hand Book 2001, Meghalaya.
3. Marak, C.R., *Influence of English on Garo Poetry*, p. 10.
4. Bhakt, G.P., *An Outline of Geography of Meghalaya*, 2nd Ed. 2002, p. 9.
5. Burling, R., Rengsanggre, *Family and Kinship in a Garo Village*, 2nd Ed. 1997. p. 21.
6. Marak, C.R., *Influence of English on Garo Poetry*. New Delhi. 1985, p. 11. 7, *Ibid.*
8. Rongmuthu, D.S., *Apasong Agana*, 1970, p. 226.
9. *Ibid.*, p. 227.
10. A. Playfair, *The Garos*, p. 10.
11. Sangma, M.S., *History of Garo Literature*, 1983, p. 1.
12. Marak, C.R., *Influence of English on Garo Poetry*, p. 13.
13. Sangma, M.S., *A-chikkuni Ma-ambi*, 1995, p. 15.
14. Carey, W., *The Garo Jungle Book*, p. 11.
15. *Ibid.*, p. 14.
16. Sangma, M.S., *History of Garo Literature*, p. 1.
17. *Ibid.*, p. 2.
18. *Ibid.*
19. Sangma, M.S, *History of Garo Literature*, p. 2.
20. Kar, P.C. *The Glimpses of The Garos*. p. 29.
21. Marak, L.R., Pa Togan. *Nengminja Sangma*, (*Kan-dikgipa Dakmesokani*) pp. 1-2.; Momin, K.W.: *Assam aro Meghalayani Katta* (*A History of Assam and Meghalaya*) Revised Ed. 1980, pp. 152-53.
22. Sangma, M.S., *A-chikkuni Maambi*, p. 22.
23. Sangma, M.S., *History of Garo Literature*, pp. 5-6.
24. Marak, J.L.R., *Balpakram*. (*The Land of Spirits Garo Mythology*), p. 4.

Chapter II

Relief Operations

During 1960's and 1970's large number of people left erstwhile East Pakistan to seek shelter in the adjoining areas of the India Union. Garo Hills District is situated on the international border, north of the Mymensing district. Many of them were rehabilitated along the plain belt of north-West Garo Hills and also some parts of Nokma Aking[1] during the years 1964, 1965 and 1966. At present they are spread all over Garo Hills District.

Garo Hills lie next to the international border, north of Mymensing District, and immediately East of the extremely porous Goalpara District, through which the immense stretch of Brahmaputra and its tributaries flow into Bangladesh. As the area is contiguous, so is the population structure. On the other side of the international border live the same communities with similar tradition and dialects, in different proportion like the Garo, Koch, Hajong, Hindu, Banai, Dalu and Muslim communities. When unrest and persecution occurs, great numbers of all these communities cross over the border and take refuge in Garo Hills where they meet and merge with their own community. This aspect of kinship definitely plays a part as they are assured of the sympathy. No reports of absorption harassment or repression of their community in India have been heard. Some of them went straight to their relatives without informing the authorities. For this reason, the detailed statistics about the number of refugees is not clearly known and is never clearly reflected in the official entries.

Although human movement from Bangladesh to Garo Hills continued after independence, major influx took place in the year 1964 and 1971.

In January 1964, due to social, political and communal unrest, many minority groups from Sylhet and Mymensing districts streamed into the eastern tip of India like Tripura, Mizoram and Meghalaya.

Number of Refugee Camps in 1964

During 1964 mass exodus there were nine transit camps under Dalu area of Garo Hills District. These camps were on the Indo-Bangladesh border belt of Garo Hills, namely:

(i) Machangpani
(ii) Bhogai
(iii) Chandabhoi
(iv) Bilkona
(v) Deplipara

(vi) Dalu
(vii) Magupara
(viii) Mineng, and
(ix) Dindini.

Other transit camps were Baghmara, Sibbari and Purakhasia etc. The refugees were shifted from those above mentioned camps to other interior camps, like Rongnabak, Ganol and Rongram of the Garo Hills District and to Matia Molonggaud Panchali area of Goalpara District of Assam[1,2] in these interior Refugee Relief Camps (R.R Camp). Displaced persons were retained till they were fully rehabilitated. The Ganol camp of 1964 was closed down in September 1974 which was the last R.R. Camp.

Number of Refugee Camps in 1971

During Bangladesh liberation war of 1971, many refugees took shelter on the Indo-Bangladesh border of Garo hills of Meghalaya. Government of India, Department of Relief and Rehabilitation provided relief camps for the Bangladeshi and local evacuees. There were 16 (sixteen) camps in Garo Hills. They are:

(i) Dalu Vety Compound
(ii) Chandabhoi
(iii) Sisengpara
(iv) Halchati
(v) Machangpani
(vi) Dimapara

(vii) Mineng
(viii) Bilkona
(ix) Sibbari
(x) Baghmara
(xi) Purakasia
(xii) Ampati
(xiii) Mahendragauj
(xiv) Kalaipara
(xv) Patizora and
(xvi) Chibinang

According to Roosevelt Ch. Momin there are V.I.P. Relief camp at Sangsanggre near Tura of Garo Hills where Political Leaders are accommodated.[3]

Communities and their Approximate Number at Various Camps in 1964

In 1964 influx, the refugees were not only Garos but also there were other communities like Bengali, Bihari, Koch, Banai, Raj Bongshi, Dalu, Hajong etc. Their approximate number can be seen below:

The Table 2.2 shows that out of 82,132 there were 32,640 Garos, 19,619 Bengalis, 13,842 Hajongs, 5,584 Biharis, 4,117 Koches, 3,227 Dalus, 1,243 Raj Bongshis, 906 Banais 582 Cobblers, 246 Fishermen, 96 Sweepers and 30 Barbers. Moreover it was mentioned in the statement that "It is very difficult to give the correct figure of the refugees as many refugees took shelter with their relatives etc. without giving any information to their camps. Some refugees were known to have directly gone to the plains of their own accord".[4]

The refugees were shifted from the camps to other parts of the district and to outside the district especially in the plains like Matia, Dudhnoi and Srirampur of Goalpara district. Within the District they were shifted to Rongnabok, Ganol and Rongram Relief camps.

Refugees shifted from Dalu transit camps to other places, since November 1964 up to the 8th February, 1965 are as follows:

Table 2.1

To	Dudhnoi	in	November,	1964	=	1,057 Nos
To	Srirampur	in	December,	1964	=	84 Nos
To	Srirampur	in	January,	1965	=	272Nos
To	Srirampur	in	February,	1965	=	143 Nos
	Grand Total				=	1,556 Nos

It was also mentioned in Annexure – 'b' of GRRO – 10/65/3423-27 dated 8th April, 1965, that 4068 refugees were released to their relatives from Dalu Relief Camp.

The numbers of refugees in Rongram Relief camp were around 5,197 as on 20-06-1964, out of which Garo Christian Agriculturists were 3,207 and Non-Agriculturists 255 with a total of 3,462. Garo Non-Christians 1,698 and Non-Agriculturists 37, total being 1,735.

In Ganol Relief Camp population of refugees as on 24-10-1964 was around 4,195 (Table 2.3).

Table 2.2: Community Wise Break up of Refugees at Various Camps Under Dalu Area in 1964

Sl. No.	Name of Refuges Camps	*General*		*Backwrd Classes*				*Scheduled Caste*				*Scheduled Tribe*		
		Bengali	*Bihari*	*Koach*	*Banai*	*Raj Bongshi*	*Dalu*	*Barber*	*Sweeper*	*Fisher man*	*Cobbler*	*Garo*	*Hajongs*	*Total*
1.	Machanagpani	322	26	201	21	—	701	30	5	47	25	4008	1638	7024
2.	Bhogai	450	297	—	67	170	683	—	—	—	8	3958	1336	7077
3.	Chandabhoi	6	16	474	—	2	48	—	9	9	9	609	1626	2849
4.	Ilkona	306	43	—	332	—	9	—	—	—	—	5319	1158	7167
5.	Deplipara	29	—	—	—	5	—	—	—	—	—	1400	1042	2476
6.	Magupara	438	—	2304	481	37	710	—	16	16	6	1429	3829	9291
7.	Mineng	163	201	120	—	26	1051	—	66	66	34	3506	129	5296
8.	Dindini	—	—	27	5	—	25	—	—	—	—	7392	20	7469
9.	Dalu	17905	5001	991	—	1003	—	—	—	—	500	5019	3064	33483
	Total	**19619**	**5584**	**4117**	**906**	**1243**	**3227**	**30**	**96**	**96**	**582**	**32640**	**13842**	**82132**

Table 2.3

	Agriculture	*Non-Agriculture*	*Total*
Garo Christian	3,185	38	3,123
Garo Non Christian	1,010	42	1,072
Total	4,215	80	4,195

After rehabilitation some refugees in the month of April and May 1966 comprised of 380 families with 1,598 persons in Ganol Camp.

The people in Rongnabok R.R. Camp were 8,243 as on 14-11-1964, of which were Garo Christians 7,619, Garo Non-Christians 590 and Hindus only 34.

Some refugees from Rongram, Ganol and Rongnabak camp were shifted to Matia and other neighboring places of Goalpara District of Assam. It was mentioned by one of the displaced persons of erstwhile East Pakistan that in Matia camp there were six camps and the number of persons were around sixty to seventy five thousand. Many Garo refugees and other communities were shifted to Goalpara and other district of Assam. It was told that by the same person that Bengali refugees were shifted to Boko camp of Assam. In 1967-68 some Garo refugees were brought back from Matia to Ganol camp.

Classification According to Religion at Various Camps in 1971

In 1971 Bangladesh Liberation war sixteen Relief Camps were set up in Garo Hills District for Bangladeshi evacuees and also for Local Evacuees. Religion wise their numbers at varied camps are given in the Table 2.4.

Table 2.4

(As on 7-8-1971)

Sl. No.	*Name of Camps*	*Hindus*	*Muslims*	*Others*	*Total*
1.	Dalu (Barenggapara)	1,352	6	366	1,724
2.	Vety. Compound Dalu	3,930	1,037	1,286	6,253
3.	Chandabhoi	5,573	1,156	1,290	8,019
4.	Sisengpara	2,985	852	1,799	5,636
5.	Halchati	2,125	2	584	2,711
6.	Machangpam	3,958	26	939	4,923
7.	Dimapaia	5,037	1,934	8,352	15,323
8.	Puraldiasia	5,086	737	2,100	7,923
9.	Baghmara	34,682	2,772	16,390	53,844
10.	Sibbad	7,138	1713	5864	14715
11.	Bilkona	48	3604	4022	7674
12.	Mineng	433	1971	5124	7528
13.	Mahendraganj				
14.	Kalaipara	15,637	7,929	490	24,056
15.	Patijora				
16.	Ampati	3,074	8,221	12	11307
	Total	**91,058**	**31,960**	**48,618**	**1,71,636**

As on 7-8-1971 there were 1,71,636 in sixteen camps. Baghmara had the highest number with 53,844 refugees. The Hindus numbered 91,058, Muslims 31,960 and others 48,618.

In 1971, evacuees started to take shelter in Garo Hills from 26/03/71 onward till February 1972. Daily record shows that there was continuous flow of the evacuees since 26/03/71 which lasted up to 9/12/71. It was found that the maximum number recorded was around 2,82,947, as on 9-12-1971.

Report of the Refugees in different camps of the Garo Hills up to 9/12/71 received from S.P Office, Garo Hills, Tura is given in Table 2.5.

Table 2.5

Name of the camp	Non-Muslim	Muslim	Christian	Total
Dalu	49546	19507	21800	90853
Bafihmara	72926	3631	15867	92424
Mahendraganj	20925	14846	490	36261
Ampau	4861	9558	12	14431
Sibbari	31831	2180	5172	39183
Purakhasia	5196	2494	2105	9795
Total	**1,85,285**	**52,216**	**45,446**	**2,82,947**

Out of 2,82,947, the number of Non Muslims were 1,85,285, Muslims 52,216 and the Christians 45,446. After registration 54,494 were released to stay with their friends and relatives.

Indian Evacuees at Various Camps in 1971

During the events leading to Bangladesh Liberation War in 1971 Indian evacuees were also accommodated in camps. The figure of the Bangladesh evacuees and the Indian evacuees are given in Table 2.6.

Condition of Camps

Many relief camps were temporarily constructed with the locally available materials (i.e. by small woods and bamboos). Construction works was given to the contractors. Some refugees were employed on construction camps on wages. In some places school buildings and other government buildings were also used for camps. It has been mentioned that some camps were not in good condition.

Table 2.6

(As on 29-11-1971)

Sl. No.	*Name of Camps*	*Bangladeshi*	*Indian*	*No. of Indian Families*
1.	Veterinary Compound (Dalu)	6,352	10874	1914
2.	Chandabhoi	8,684	(not available)	(not recorded)
3.	Halchat	2,735	271	53
4.	Machangpani	5,149	1727	(not recorded)
5.	Dimapara	14,126	2,700	214
6.	Purakhasia	9,674	301	39
7.	Sesengpara	5,518	1,146	237
8.	Mineng	8,941	3,061	715
9.	Bilkona	10,255	3070	474
10.	Sibbari	40,009	2,615	352
11.	Baghmara	69,856	4,198	679
12.	Kalaipara	17610	No evacuees.	(Not recorded)
13.	Patijora	10,989	10,973	
14.	Ampati	11,552	22	(not recorded)
15.	Chibinang	6,957	No evacuees.	
	Total	**2,28,404**	**40,958**	**4,682**

One of the problems was of leaking roofs. Although the Government provided tarpaulins but they were not sufficient to cover all the roofs.

The Table 2.7 for the construction of relief camps for the Bangladesh Refugees during the year 1971, shows the particulars about the organization.

Every camp was administered by a camp commandant appointed by the Government with the official designation of Assistant Relief and Rehabilitation Officer (A.R.R.O). They were assisted by the Lower Division Assistants. To maintain law and order police personels were also given to them. They were incharge of distribution of relief rations

Table 2.7

Sl. No.	Name of Camps	No. of Camps for Refugees	No. of Administrative Buildings	No. of Latrines.
1.	Dimapara	273	19	—
2.	Chandabhoi	44	—	—
3.	Patijora	157	29	66
4.	Kalaipara	156	21	37
5.	Sangknigri	274	40	—
6.	Chibinang	332	40	—
7.	Nawalgre	367	40	—
8.	Balalgre	244	40	—
9.	Nunmati	272	40	—
10.	Ampati	326	—	314
11.	Mineng	734	—	415
12.	Bilkona	426	—	524
13.	Sibbari	1130	—	690
14.	Baghmara	320	—	485
15.	Dalu Vety.Compound	64	—	144
16.	Machangpani I	112	—	200
17.	Machangpani II	101	—	240
18.	Machangpani III	28	—	95
19.	Purakhasia	220	—	506
20.	Sisengpara	62	—	313
21.	Dalu High School Ground	—	—	—
22.	Goabari	464	—	—
	Total	**6106**	**269**	**4104**

for the refugees. They had power to settle disputes among the refugees. In 1971, Crunden S. Sangma, A.R.R.O. of Sibbari told about a problem in administration that during in his absence the refugees broke the godown and three persons died. It happened while they were fighting for relief rations. J.P. Singh, the ADM of Tura, sent him a message to immediately to reach his camp immediately. One section of C.R.P.F. was sent with him. He threatened not to supply them ration for a week. Later they came and begged his forgiveness.

Every member of the camp had orders to maintain discipline and cleanliness. Government provided drinking water facilities in every camp.[6] The list of Tube well and Ring wells installed in various R.R Camps in 1971 is as per Table 2.8.

Table 2.8

Sl. No.	*Camps*	*No. of Ring wells*	*No. of Tube wells*	*Pipe/Water/ Taps.*
1.	Bhatna	6	6	—
2.	Kacharipara	2	10	—
3.	Dimapara	14	3	—
4.	Bilkona	—	57	—
5.	Patijora	—	50	—
6.	Sangknigri	3	—	—
7.	Halchati	3	—	—
8.	Dalu	5		—
9.	Ampati	2	20	—
10.	Mineng	2	3	65
11.	Balalgre	—	5	—
12.	Numnati	—	20	—
13.	Sesengpara	—	25	—
14.	Kalaipaia	—	47	—
15.	Chibinang	—	15	—
16.	Sibbari	2	20	138
17.	Baghmara	—	20	—
18.	Chandabhoi	—	20	—
19.	Mahendraganj	—	4	—
20.	Machangpani	—	20	—
	Total	**42**	**365**	**203**

The following Statement is the record of Medical facilities and Public Health Measure taken for Refugees in Meghalaya up to October 1971.

Statement

1. Number of Doctors employed = 23
2. Number of para-medical staff engaged = 24
3. Number of Medical students engaged = 8
4. Medical Stores supply Depots functioning = 1
5. Number of Bullet injury case treated = 32
6. Number of persons inoculated = 526+237
   (Ino & boosting dose)
7. Number of persons vaccinated (Pv and Rv) = 332 & 137
8. Epidemic of Cholera, Gastro-enteritis and other diseases.
9. Number of patients treated for various diseases 7,77,776.[7]

	Attack	No. of Persons	Death
(i)	Cholera and Gastro-entritis	2707	1480
(ii)	Chicken Pox	144	Nil
(iii)	Diphtheria	Nil	Nil
(iv)	Pneumonia and Bronchitis	321	178
(v)	Measles	9	Nil
(vi)	Others	952	644
	Total Death		2302

Source: Civil Surgeon, Garo Hills Tura.

Mortality

The Medical report of the Civil Surgeon of Tura says that the total number of deaths were 2,302. From which 1,480 died of Cholera and Gastro-enteritis 178 of Pneumonia and bronchitis 644 of other diseases since 26-03-1971 upto the Month of October, 1971 in the RR. Camps of Garo Hills.

According to Mitra N. Sangma of Nehru A-ding, Tura, a former A.R.R.O. of Mineng Relief camp in 1971, there were many sick persons in his camp. Some of them were suffering from malaria, diarrhoea and Gastro-enteritis and many died of those diseases. Everyday 5 to 10 persons died in his camp.

During 1964 influx, on account of over crowding in the camp in Rongnabak, there were sometimes 10 to 15 and sometimes 10 to 20 deaths daily. It was mentioned by one of the displaced persons that they could not even give them a proper burial.

It was learnt from Dewanshing S. Rongmurthu's complaint letter about keeping refugees in Baghmara that sometimes the refugees buried corpses in 2 to 3 deep ft. pits. At night tigers came to eat them, which caused a great deal of public nuisance. Sometimes they threw the corpses into the Simsang river.

Relief Work and Voluntary Organizations

The Indian Red Cross Society

This organization first started its operations in the early part of June, 1971. At first it opened a dispensary at Machangpani and side by side a milk feeding centre was also started for the benefit of children, expectant and lactating mothers and aged persons. Gradually this organisation's activities were extended from 1 to 53 milk feeding centers and for emergency measures 2 (two) transit hospitals were opened with the help of Iris Medical team, of which one was at Dimapara and another was at Machangpani. Another medical unit was opened at Sibbari. Besides, this organization distributed blankets, jerseys and second hand clothes etc. By the month of November 1971, it have covereds all the camps.

The Rama Krishna Mission

Its operations were at Chandabhoi camp, which started from 8 August 1971 and ended on 22nd January 1972. It had its own dispensary. This organization also assisted in a milk feeding centre in the camp, distributing baby food, barley and Glucose. It also ran a primary school.

Evangelical Fellowship of India Committee on Relief (EL.F.LC.O.R.)

This organization operated in mainly two camps i.e. Sisengpara and Halchati. They conducted two medical dispensaries at these camps and ran a camp hospital at Sisengpara. They gave a very devoted and efficient service. It distributed blankets, sarees, dhotis, petticoats, clothes, markin (grey) pieces, vests etc.

Garo Baptist Convention and North Goalpara Garo Baptist Union

Both the organizations distributed clothings. Garo Baptist Convention distributed sarees, dhotis and flannel etc. at Purakhasia camp and other Unions distributed clothing at Baghmara.

Christian Agency for Social Action (C.A.S.A.)

C.A.S.A.'s relief activities were engaged in distributing clothing, blankets and giving primary medical help at Kalaipara and Ampati Camps.

CARITAS[8]

This organization started operating from Machangpani camp in the month of November 1971. They also distributed sarees; blankets, dhotis, soap and utensils to the camps at Bhkona, Diaaapara, Mineng, Dalu, Ampati, Kalaipara and Patijora.

During Bangladesh Liberation War in 1971 Shillong branch of fhe Ramakrishna Mission participated in the Bangladesh relief operation in Dawki sector of Khasi Hills and in Tura sector of Garo Hills, Meghalaya. In Tura sector, the Mission took the charge of medical, educational and cultural works along with milk, clothing and garment distribution among the evacuees in the Chandabhoi camp. This Mission spent from its own fund Rs. 48,696.76 for Tura sector excluding the valuation of relief materials.[9]

Camp: Chandabhoi (Under Tura Sector)

Period of Work: 8th August, 1971 to 22nd January 1972.

Number of refugees: 8,790.

Medical Work

The Ramakrishna Mission had its own well equipped dispensary of the camp site Chandabhoi itself. The Mission had two qualified resident doctors and other full-time para-medical staff in the camp. It ran two Homeopathic OPDs under a qualified Homeo doctor. Small surgical cases were also taken up in the Mission dispensary. Number of patients treated during the period were 57,099.

Milk Distribution

The Ramakrishna Mission ran 2 milk canteens in the camp daily. The Mission workers distributed prepared milk with sugar among the refugee children, nursing mothers, patients and other needy persons, on medical advice.

Quantity of Milk powder consumed	:	3125 Kgs.
Quantity of Sugar consumed	:	499.25 Kgs.
No. of Units of prepared milk	:	1,41,905
Baby food, Barley and Glucose Quantities consumed		
Baby food	:	997.97 Kgs.
Glucose	:	9.22 Kgs.

Educational and Cultural

The Ramakrishna Mission rendered service in the form of supplying of text books etc. to a primary school established in the Chandabhoi camp which had 268 children and 12 teachers. Text books supplied: 350 Nos.

The Mission also conducted various social functions and celebrations like Christmas, Durga Pujia, Kali Puja, Moharram, Independence Day (15th August), etc. as also the birthday of Holy mother and Swami Vivekananda in the camp for the benefit of the refugee inmates. Daily prayers and Kirtanak, etc. were also conducted.

The Mission distributed the following articles amongst the needy refugees in the camp.

New Sarees	:	2,557 pieces.
New Dhoties	:	1,308 pieces.
New Shirts	:	1,269 pieces.
New Pants	:	1,856 pieces.
New Frocks	:	1,439 pieces.
New Napkins	:	85 pieces.
New Blouses	:	338 pieces.
New Woollen Blankets	:	1,000 pieces.
New Cotton Blankets	:	2,989 pieces.
Old Clothes and garments	:	1,826 pieces.

Materials like blankets dhotis, sarees, soap and garments distributed in different camps by the different voluntary organizations are given below:

Table 2.9

Camp	*Cotton Blankets*	*Dhoties*	*Saries*	*Soaps*	*Cotton Dress*	*Woolen Blankets*
Machangpani	1669	1277	1841	5744	5560	1680
Dalu Veterinary	2167	1514	1910	5592	4918	690
Dimapara	4557	2186	3875	10984	5656	1100
Mineng	2272	1574	2649	8416	7360	696
Bilkona	3070	2250	3475	11100	8912	972
Chibinang	2679	2542	2989	9052	4818	441
Ampati	—	6014	4700	16428	6152	—
Patijora	4118	3809	3442	16038	6592	—
JCalaipam	3944	3568	3460	13984	4006	—
Total	**23792**	**24734**	**28338**	**97338**	**53974**	**5479**

Among the voluntary organizations, rendering relief work in Garo Hills district CARITAS proved a dedicated organization. (Vide letter No. TRN. 12/72/Pt –2 /92. Dtd. The 6th July 1972).

Laws Concerning Registration of Refugees

All refugees coming from Bangladesh and taking shelter in India must get themselves registered in terms of the order issued by the Government of India under Foreigner Registration Act, 1946.

All such refugees must have a valid registration card in their possession issued by the Registration Authority in which the place and the period are mentioned for them to stay in India. Registration certificates are issued by the police officer attached to the Relief Camp.

Those who come to Assam and Meghalaya as a result of political unrest in Bangladesh must get themselves registered.

The state government fixed the 1st December 1971 as the last date by which the refugees were to complete the registration work including endorsement on certificate in regard to the period of validity.[10]

In 1971, temporary permits were given to a large number of East Pakistani evacuees to stay in the adjoining areas of the Indian Union.

Right after registration of their names ration cards were issued to each family on the basis of which they were issued Rice, Mustard Oil, Dal and other necessary things by the Government.

Opportunities given to the Refugees

In 1964 influx there were Lower primary and Upper primary schools opened by the Government for refugee children in Rongram and Rongnabok Relief Camps. Teachers were appointed from amongst the educated refugees. After their rehabilitation those schools were transferred from Rongram to Nidanpur[11] and from Rongnabak to Balachanda, Chochokia. Shri Wilson. Rechil of Balachanda, one of the displaced persons of East Pakistan was working in that school till his retirement. Right after coming from East Pakistan he was given the work of Moharar (sectional assistant) in P.W.D. and was sent to Matia Goalpara, but he resigned from that service and came back to work as a teacher in the same year. Each of the four teachers were given Rs. 125/- per month in Rongnabak Refugee Relief M-E School. School text books were provided freely by the Government as well as N.G.Os for school children.

Many young men were recruited for Assam Rifles and West Bengal Rifles from amongst refugees while they were in the camps. One Ex-serviceman Mina Kumar Rechil from Williampur, was recruited from Rongnabak camp.

Those who were willing to do further studies were given opportunity to study freely in the colleges. Many young men and women studied in Union Christian College. Some of them are still working at the Directorate level under the Government of Meghalaya, some of them are working in Garo Hills Autonomous District Council. One Tapan Marak is at present Land Settlement Officer in G.H.A.D.C. Bikash Rechil of 1964 batch of refugees, residing at, Tura Tetenkkol rose in the services as civil officer, and retired as Deputy Commissioner of Baghmara, South Garo Hills District, in November, 2001.

Those who did not receive agricultural land were given business loan under small trader scheme. By far the most common means of rehabilitation by the Government of India was to provides reclaimed land for agriculture to settle down. Families were allotted farmland, a pair of bullocks, homestead plots and other items under different schemes.

References

1. Marak, Grohonsing A., *The Bangladesh and The Background*, Unpublished Document, p. 2.2.
2. *Ibid.*
3. Rhoosevelt Ch. Momin, *Bonepa A-tiBa, Tura,* Retired M.C.S. Officer and ARRO, on 08-03-2002,
4. Videleter No. 10/65/3423-27 dated 8th April, 1965 from EDO to the Deputy Secretary, Rehabilitation, Ministry of Rehabilitation, Government of India.
5. Vide Memo No. GRRO-7/64-65/3253 Dtd. Dalu fee 8th February, 1965.
6. Vide memo. No. MPHE/TRA/2340/Dated 26/6/72.
7. Vide Memo. No. Refugee R/71/10,009 Dated Tura the 17th November, 1971.
8. '*Caritas*' is a Sanskrit word, meaning 'Charity Work'. Henre it refers to relief services for the poor, needy irrespective of caste, creed and religion especially during cyclone aid earthquake etc. Caritas was organized by Calholic Bishops' Conference. It is also known as Catholic Relief Services (C. R. S.).
9. Vide letter No. EBR/117/72 Dtd. 10th June 1972 from Ramakrishna Mission Secretary Swomi Abjajananda to the Deputy Commissioner, Khasi Hills District
10. Vide Press note. No. 76, Shfllong Nov. 17th 1971.
11. Wilson Rechil of Balachanda, West Garo Hills, Meghalaya on 29-01-2002.

Chapter III

Cross Border Movement—Causes

Since Independence, groups and individuals from erstwhile East Pakistan (present Bangladesh) having been crossing over to India. The Bangladeshi influx along the Indo-Bangladesh border like West Bengal, Assam, Meghalaya, Tripura and Mizoram continues to create socio-economic and political problems.

In 1964, 82,132 number of East Pakistani refugees crossed the border and were staying in Garo Hills and some pockets of Assam. Even in 1971 large number of Bangladesh evacuees crossed the border and took shelter on the soil of Garo Hills. At that time although some were repatriated, and many others were deported by the Government of India, but many continued to over stay. It can be seen from the news paper that there are reports of large scale illegal influx of Bangladeshi national who manage to infiltrate into the country in spite of checks and controls at the international border on account of long, open and porous nature of the border.[1]

In this study the causes of movement into Garo Hills mainly in 1964 and in 1971 have been taken up and the resons why in those periods huge number of influx took place? What reasons compelled them to cross the border and which made them to stay in Garo Hills.

The causes of the flight of 1964 are also recorded in the available documents. Besides, various reasons have been given by different persons who have been staying in Garo Hills, since 1964.

Following are the causes as available from the recorded documents and given by different people from the earstwhile East Pakistan and those who have been staying in Garo Hills.

After the formation of Pakistan cases of frequent rioting, looting and robbery occurred. These were made by the Majority (i.e. Muslims) on the minorities in North Mymensing district "All the immovable properties of the Minority Communities were looted, burnt and movable properties were forcibly taken away by the majority Community in East Pakistan. The immigrants were not allowed to bring their jewelleries and other immovable properties into India by the East Pakistani authorities"[2] Serial number 14(a) of the same set says: "the attitude of the East Pakistan authority was not favourable to the Minority Community" (b) "The opportunities of employment in private and in Government services were almost blocked" on account of to these reasons and huge number of East Pakistani minorities left their home and took shelter in Garo Hills during 1960s.

Bikash Marak Rechil spoke on the causes of mass Influx in 1964.[3] According to him right after the partition harassment was started over the minorities by the majority. During 1960s this situation turned to worse. The Muslims ill-treated A-chiks, Hajongs, Koches Banais, Dalus and Bengalis, and most of the time victims were women. Many movable and non-movable properties of minorities were looted; houses were set on fire by the Muslims. He stated that he himself was one of the persons who rushed to the spot to help while dacoity was being committed on the houses of the Dalus of Gusbell village. If they opposed they were killed. If they filed a petition against the looters and dacoits or reported the matter to the police their appeals were ignored. The cause lies in the expulsion of Muslims from Bihar state of India. Many Muslims refugees from Bihar were present in the adjacent villages. The Government of Pakistan, in order to give the land of the minorities to Muslim refugees from Bihar, indirectly encouraged persecution because ordinary citizens could not use guns to shoot minority communities. In Mymensing alone there were around 40,000 Muslim refugees from Bihar. They were brought during the night into the lands abandoned by the minority communities.

Bikas R. Marak also heard the rumour being spread that 'they were taking revenge on the minority of East Pakistan for the destruction of a Muslims shrine in Kashmir'.

Grohonsing A. Marak stated in his unpublished manuscript, "The Bangladesh in the Background" that in January 1964, large ghastly killing of minority groups in East Bengal, the victims were Bengalis, Garos, Koches,

Hajongs, Dalus, Banais etc. As a consequence number of East Pakistani refugees streamed into the eastern tip of India viz. Tripura, Mizoram and Meghalaya.[4]

Amarendra Simsang Sangma's (an immigrant of 1951) hailed from Amindagre village of Garo Hills District.[5] He came from Birisiri of Bangladesh. He stated that in East Pakistan they were treated as second class citizens. Secondly, there they had a feeling of insecurity and they had to face various obstacles in earning their livelihood. By comparison, in India if they were educated it was very easy to get jobs in Garo Hills in those days.

He crossed over the border alone and later his parents joined him. They lived in his grandparent's home. His parents left for Cooch Bihar to work at Tin Hata Mission. He passed matriculation in 1951 just before coming to Garo Hills. In Garo Hills he served in the Community Development Block as Gram Sevak since 1955. In 1964 influx, he worked as Assistant Relief and Rehabilitation Officer.

He stated that the majority community used to molest minority girls, tried to marry them forcibly and tried to convert them into Muslims. They looted their property and lands. Sometimes young men were arrested and tortured. They used to harass mainly the uneducated.

They also used to harass mainly A-chiks and Hajongs since they regarded Hajongs as Communists and A-chiks as anti Pakistani. In the border, the minorities who lived along the border of Mymensing district struggled for amalgmation of their land with India. The Garos took the leading part in this movement. The movement started right after British left India and that time onwards the Muslims took a dislike for the Garos. The situations became more intense during 1960s. During those days they used to drive out all the minority communities from East Pakistan.

Dinesh Chandra Sangma[6], migrating from Birespur village of erstwhile East Pakistan, went to Calcutta to study law. From there he was invited by late Captain W.A. Sangma to work as Secretary in Garo Hills District Council. His father late Jinga Marak was from Boldamgre village of Garo Hills District. He came to Garo Hills to stay permanently. His family came to Garo Hills before the riot. His family, too, left their home but not as accused for rioting. Their area was not affected, but mostly the northern borders of Mymensing district were. Many people fled from that area during 1964 riots. In 1964, mass exodus took place, due to the atrocities committed by the Muslims. Many people left their home and country panic-stricken.

Regarding the major influx of 1964, Ananta Sangma[7] has narrated his experiences which started from Haluaghat on a market day. (Markets were held every Thursday). Utter confusion started from that market place when the East Pakistan Riffles started random firing. In panic, people started to flee into Garo Hills, because in those areas most of the inhabitants were A-chiks, Hajongs, Koches, Dalus and other minority communities. The areas mostly affected were the border areas like Boral Gandi, Kasot Gandi. Many Hajongs and Koches living today on the Southern border of Garo Hills would reply to the question as to how they happened to be living in those areas, that they had fled from Haluaghat, from Naltabari Birisiri, Durgapur and other villages. The A-bima of Bangladesh inhabited by

Garos is located in an interior area which is around 100 km. away from Indo-Bangladesh border, was not much effected by the rioting. He observed that the Muslims living near A-bima were very good compared with those living in the border areas. He observed that Muslims of East Pakistan wanted only Muslim Community to live in their country. Even political leaders indirectly supported them in their acts of persecution.

Monoronjon Sangma[8] came from Barua village of East Pakistan in 1964. He narrated that their paddy, cattle and other movable properties were taken away forcibly by the Muslims. Many times they were asked to leave their places. They were repeatedly threatened that if they would not vacate their lands and homes they would be killed. That was the reason why many of them left.

Horesh Mankin Sangma migrated with his wife Smt. Bosilla Dajel Marak[9] in 1964. He hailed from Kanai village situated about 25 miles from Lido-Bangladesh borderer and his wife hails from Chondokona village of near Sibbari under Haluaghat Police Station. They spoke mournfully of the reasons for their departure; they recalled that they were treated inhumanly by the Muslims. Women and girls were abducted and their honours and dignity were violated by the Muslims. Their goods were looted and their lawful ploughlands were forcibly occupied and cattle lifted. Although lawful complaints filed by them for these, in the court of law or in the Police Station no legal action was taken by the authorities concerned against the culprits.

Just before coming to India, Smt. Bosilla Marak stated, that Hajongs and Garo's villages were set to fire by Muslims with the help of the East Pakistan Rifles. For these antisocial elements, which were causing deep apprehension and anxiety, compelled them to leave their country.

Noho Rechil Marak and his wife Smt. Beronika Mankin Sangma[10] came from Monchapara of East Pakistan in 1964. They told that hundreds of Muslim refugees from Assam dispersed along the border where mostly inhabited by tribal people. To give shelter to those displaced persons from Assam, East Pakistan Government drove out non-Muslims minorities indirectly from border strip of North Mymensing district.

Muslims refugees of Assam looted their properties, robbed their paddies from their granaries, their cattle were lifted and womenfolk were molested and girls were kidnapped during night. Thus, they were compelled to leave their houses. As soon as they left their houses Muslim refugees occupied their house and lands.

Jotdindra Manda came from Polastala village, under Haluaghat Police Station in 1964. Before-coming to India he worked as 'Dobadhar' for 18 years (that was like the police of Union council, as he said) Under Union council there were many Garo villages, Hajongs and Koch villages, Banai villages and Dalu villages. One named Giris Pastor was also one of the members of that council. Once he went to talk to East Pakisani authorities regarding problems and difficulties of the minorities that day he was told in a negative way that they would have to give their place to the Muslims refugees of Assam.

According to Jotindra Manda[11] the Muslims from Assam started to loot the minorities even during day time, first they looted Bobonkura village the minorities and lodged a complaint with the police. They came to inspect the matter but did not take any legal action against the culprits. The same group looted the property and articles from Hajong and Koches, later they did the same to the Garos, too. He narrated the events which he saw before coming to Garo Hills. He was eye witness to Joyramkura Dalu village being set on fire by the Muslims. The inhabitants escaped somehow, but their cattle, goats, pigs, fowls and their granaries were completely burnt down. The people were afraid to live any longer, so the people of seven villages left their homes and lands and proceeded to Garo Hills.

Sotindra Chisim[12] came from Joyrampara village which was under Noltabari Thana of East Pakistan, in 1964. He said that Muslim, burnt the houses during night; sometimes they looted their property during day time. Woman and young girls were molested. On account of these persecutions many people left for Garo Hills. He asked himself if others were fleeing, why should he stay back alone? After a long thought he came with them, too. He witnessed that Garos, Hajongs and Koches were the first to flee.

According to him the main causes of the persecution was the political movement among the Hajongs and Koches. These two communities joined the communist party and they threatened to break the thanas, for this reason the police threatened to arrest them in return. The Muslims were of the opinion that if they tolerated the aggressive behavior of the Hajongs and Koches, some day they might harm the Muslims community. Due to this feeling of insecurity they drove out Hajongs and Koches.

The Garos were not victims of such ejections, but out of fear that the same fate might befall on them in future, they fled from their country in anticipation of persecutions.

Mina Kumar Rechil,[13] came from Phulgo Akonpara, which is under Haluaghat Police Station. This village is around 2 to 3 km. away from border. He was around 15 or 16 years old when he came along with others to Garo Hills in 1964. The reasons he quoted for leaving their homeland was that since 1958 General Ayub Khan began to oppress the minorities in East Pakistan. During 1960s the oppressions became more severe than ever before. They did not drive them out directly but used anti-social elements to eject them. During the year of entry (i.e. in 1964) one Dalu village, Joyramkura, where around 200 to 250 families were living was set on fire by the Muslims. In that episode it seemed that East Pakistan Rifles joined the common people or else people could not dare to do such a criminal act against such a large village. People escaped miraculously but their cattle, paddy and all other properties were burnt to ashes. The people of nearby villages gathered together and lodged a complaint with the police; but he did not see any action taken by them. It seemed that they wanted to make East Pakistan purely Islamic state with only Muslims as inhabitants. Religious intolerance seemed to be one of the chief causes of oppression and an ejection of non-Muslims out of the country.

After Independence social and political unrest broke out and huge loss was incurred by the inhabitants of the border area. There occurred great loss for inhabitants of Garo community on the Indo-East Pakistan border area. When partition between India and Pakistan took place;

many Garo villages came under East Pakistan. People of those villages wanted to amalgamate their villages with Indian Union. For that purpose they formed one organization known as A-chikna Chilchakani Kotok (The Garo Welfare Organisation) in 1951, of which Dewanshing S. Rongmuthu was the President, who undertook all the correspondence with the government. For the same purpose another organization was also formed known as *ADIVASI SANGRAM PARISAD* by the Garo People with other minorities of those areas.

Their main demand was the amalgamation of six *thanas* (Police station) which were under Shusung and Sherpur Pargana of Mymensing district, under those six thanas were The lands of the Garos, namely (i) Kalumakanda (ii) Dulgapur (iii) Haluaghat (iv) Noltabari (Taraganj) (v) Sribbardi and Serpur fell. Their demand was based on the Government of India Act, 1935 (Section 91) where it was stated, "Into this area, then under jungle the Garos came some 150 years ago. They were the first to open the country"[14] Mr. Dewansing S. Rongmuthu wrote a memorundam to the Honourable Prime Minister of the Indian Union Republic, Shri. Jawaharlal Nehru, on-17th January 1951, on behalf of the organizations for amalgamation of those six thanas with the Indian Union where 2001 Garos, who were staying on the aforesaid areas put their signatures.[15]

They also conveyed their earnest desire, through the Rev. V.J. White of the Australian Baptist Mission, Birisiri, place before the Partition Committee in Delhi for the amalgamation of thc strip of land in the Mymensing District, known as the Shunsung and Sherpur Parganas and comprising six *thanas* (Police station) of (i) Kalumakanda (ii) Durgapur (Shusung) (iii) Haluaghat, (iv) Naltabari (Taraganj) (v) Sribbardi and (vi) Sherpur, into the Indian Union[16] Rev. V.J. White assured Garos that he would himself do everything needful. They also trusted him but he went on furlough just before the sitting of the afore said Partition committee; and the task was entrusted to his Assistant Rev. Binoy Bhusan Sangma of the same place. "Rev. Binoy Bushan Sangma was, through Pro-Pakistan influence and by unforeseen difficulties in his way, been thwarted from carrying out the mission entrusted to him successfully, so he could not present before the Partition Committee the case of the Garos of the ancestral Garo country which the Mussalmans now occupy under Mussalman servitude, and thus he miserably failed to strike while the iron was hot[17]

It seemed that due to the above reasons the Garos of aforementioned areas were regarded as anti-Pakistani by the Muslim authorities. Probably due to this reason they wanted to drive out Garo and other communities from the strip of land of North Mymensing District in 1960s which were on the Lido-Pakistan border belt. During the 1964 communal riots, those areas were worst affected and many East Pakistanis came to Garo Hills.

When Rev. Binoy Bushan Sangma failed to present the case of the Garos before the Partition Committee the ancient land of the Garos, which was the integral and inseparable part of the main Garo land of the then Assam (now in Meghalaya) came to be included in the East Pakistan[18]. Since there was no one could present the case in a cogent manner to the Partition Committee about the needs, rights and claims of the Garos the Indo-Pakistan Boundary Tribunal did not do justice. Thus some portions of the main Garo Land were merged with the theocratic and Communal state of East Pakistan.[19]

During 1950s people of aforementioned areas, through their, organizations reiterated their demand for amalgamation of the Shusung and Sherpur Parganas of Mymensing district and the memorandum was given to the Prime Minister Shri Jawaharlal Nehru on the 17th January, 1951 and the reminder was sent on the 9th August, 1952. It seemed that their demand was never negotiated. When their demand was not fulfilled they became permanently part of East Pakistan. There they became victims of the atrocities by the Muslims in East Pakistan. There was no social, economic and political justice, no liberty of thought, expression, belief, faith and worship, no equality of status and of opportunities, no fraternity assuring the dignity of the individual and no instrument of social good and national progress for the Garos and other minority communities in East Pakistan. Shira also mentions that "countless inhuman tortures of the Garo villagers at the East Pakistan Armed Police camps and outposts for trifling offences, continued abductions, seduction and kidnappings and forcible conversions to Islam of the Garo women and girls".[21]

Regarding Human Rights, the memorandum to the Kurt Waldheim, the Secretary General of United Nations Organisation, on the 16th December, 1980, stated "In 1964, some Muslim goondas or anti-social elements, with the help of the East Pakistan Police, deliberately set fire to 128 (one hundred twenty eight) houses at village

Jayramkura, Police station Haluaghat, District Mymensing, Bangladesh, resulting in the loss of human lives, countless heads of cattle, several thousand tons of paddy in the granaries. The houses belonged to Hajongs and Koches, the minority tribal people in Bangladesh".[22] The above stated circumstances are the causes of the exodus which took place in 1964. It is mainly because of the atrocities on them that the minority people of East Pakistan fled across the border during 1964.

Causes of the Major Influx in 1971

East Pakistan was carved out from the former Indian province of Bengal and the Sylhet Districts of Assam. Although East was more populous, government was based in West Pakistan. From the very beginning of its formation, language remained the most problematic issue. Same status for Bengali language with Urdu and English was the demand and the movement involving all sections of the people of East Pakistan gave a strike call on the 21st February, 1952. On that day, police fired on a students' rally and several students died.[23] Mr. Ananta Sangma said that around four to five student leaders were shot dead and many of them were arrested by the police. Among the dead were Borkot, Salam, Chopper and others.[24]

Later on they did succeeded in their movement as Bengali language was conceded to be the official language in East Pakistan.

Mr. Ghoronsing A. Marak stated clearly, what he remembered in his unpublished documents (The Bangladesh and the Background) that in the wake of the

1962 Constitution,[25] the people of East Bengal, especially, the students protested against the imposition of the patently undemocratic Constitution and braved the repression leashed on them by the military dictatorship. Even such concessions as the recognition of both Bengali and Urdu granted by the Constitution could not reduce the vehemence of their protests, of the students and the people of East Bengal.

When repression failed to liquidate the Anti-Ayub[26] agitation, he recommended the replacement of the Bengali Script "For the sake of insulting East Bengal" and resorted to various ruthless and diversionary measures and tactics to crush his opponents. But these tactics failed to divert the attention for a democratic way of life.[27]

Ayub Khan's belief that the electoral college of the basic democrates would provide an alternative to the old 'politician' leadership was belied when it was found that in the elections to the National Assembly, which were held on non-party basis in April, 1962, almost all the elected candidates had previous party affiliations. The new assembly proved to be very defiant, its members started organizing themselves into "like minded groups" and demanded 'Democratization of the constitution'. In an attempt to liberalize the constitution, as a first step, political parties were legalized by an Act of the National Assembly'. This Act came to be known as the Political Parties Act, 1962. Ayub Khan ruled Pakistan until March 1969, when, he was deposed by General Yahya Khan.[28]

General Yahya Khan, after assuming office immediately proclaimed Martial Law through out the country and ordered the dissolution of the National and Provincial Assemblies and cabinets and placed the two wings of the country (East and West Pakistan) under the military administration. Since he assumed presidentship on March 31, 1969, and ironically enough, promised the people a return to democracy based on adult franchise, when conditions become normal. He also did radio broadcast on March 28, 1970, and promised of a legal frame work for the country's future constitution.[29]

On August 15, 1970, General Elections for the National Assembly, Scheduled for October 5, 1970, had been postponed for two months. The National Assembly was supposed to draft a Constitution for Pakistan within 120 days of its first meeting. The new Constitution was however ultimately subject to the acceptance of the President.

The elections to the National Assembly were held at last on December 7, 1970. Fighting the elections on the Six-points programme, the Awami League party led by Sheikh Mujibur Rehman won 160 out of the 162 seats from East Bengal in the National Assembly consisting of 300 members. Out of the 13 women who were to be nominated to the Assembly by the vote of elected members to fill seats reserved for them 7 from East Bengal and 6 from West Pakistan; the Awani League got all the seven seats from East Pakistan. In the Western wing. Zulfikar Ali Bhutto's Pakistan Peoples' Party secured 87 of the 138 seats. The Awani League was thus placed in a clear majority in the National Assembly.[30]

President Yahya Khan went on record to say that Sheikh Mujibur Rehman, the leader of the majority party in the National Assembly, would be the natural future Prime Minister of Pakistan.

The National Assembly was scheduled to meet and draft a new Constitution for Pakistan within the stipulated period of 120 days. To this end, the Awani League insisted on an early summoning of the National Assembly. It also set up a committee to draft the Constitution on the basis of six-points Programme for the consideration of the National Assembly. But Z.A. Bhutto's position came into sharp conflict with that of Sheikh Mujibur Rehman from the very start. He thought that if the National Assembly met and the Sheikh became the Prime Minister, he would have to sit in Opposition and even though he had won a majority in the Assembly from the Western wing he would have no place in the Government. To block this inevitable development he adopted obstructing postures. While Bhutto conceded that the provinces should have "Maximum political autonomy and equal powers", his concept of autonomy was never as wide as that of the Sheikh. He insisted on a strong centre as the authority to levy and collect taxes and control foreign trade and foreign aid without which, he thought, national economy would disintegrate. Sheikh Mujibur Rehman's concept of autonomy, on the other hand, was total and envisaged that the Federal Government of Pakistan should deal only with two subjects of defence and foreign affairs with all the residuary subjects vested in the federating States. Under this scheme of things, foreign trade and aid were to remain outside the jurisdiction of the centre. Apart from the demand for complete Autonomy for East Bengal even on the naming of the State, both the leaders widely differed. While Bhutto wanted Islam to be the State religion, the Awani League leader envisaged the establishment of a Federal Republic of Pakistan instead of an Islamic

Republic.[31] Therefore, the differences between the two leaders of the Eastern and Western Wings on these issues remained virtually unresolved.[32]

The fate of the National Assembly thus hanged in balance. Several parleys were, no doubt, held between the leaders of the two wings both in Karachi as well as in Dacca, but these led to no softening of attitudes on several controversial issues. Bhutto went to the extent of threatening a boycott of the Assembly until the Awami League agreed to adjust its six-point programme.

As a result of the firm postures adopted by the respective leaders of the two Wings, the meetings of the National Assembly which was summoned by the President to meet on March 3, 1971, was postponed sine die on March 1, 1971[33]

East Bengal rose instantly as one nation to demonstrate the people's firm determination to secure their rights and national solidarity under the leadership of Sheikh Mujibur Rehman.

The sharp reaction to the postponement of the Assembly session in East Bengal was spontaneous. People held demonstrations throughout the land to record their protest against the 'arbitrary' act of the President who, they thought, was playing into the hands of Bhutto.

The popular mood in East Bengal doubted whether the present regime in Pakistan would ever transfer power to the elected representatives of the people.

Sheikh Mujibur Rehman gave a clarion call for non-cooperation and a civil disobedience movement. The response from the people to the call was total.[35]

Awed with the wave of demonstration and the people's whole hearted support to the Awami League Leader and his historic non-cooperation movement General Yahya Khan modified his stand and announced that the meeting of the National Assembly would be held on March 25, 1971, though with the condition that no condition would be acceptable to him which provided for autonomy of a province. Sheikh Mujibur Rehman deeply resented this arbitrary decision of the President and set forth four conditions for attending the session of the National Assembly. These were (a) that the Martial law should be lifted immediately; (b) that the troops should be recalled to their barracks; (c) that an enquiry be held into the killing of demonstrators and (d) that the elected representatives of the people should be empowered to act on their behalf.[36]

In order to gain control over the deterioting situation in East Bengal and tighten the grip of his military machine over the popular forces. President Yahya Khan came to Dacca personally to hold negotiations with Sheikh Mujibur Rehman.

The negotiations which began on March 16, 1971 continued for several days and subsequently Bhutto was invited to participate in the deliberations[37].

Troops started pouring into East Bengal by air and sea and the noose around the neck of East Bengal was tightening.[38] (Six shiploads of West Pakistani troops landed at Chittagong and Khulna during the talks between President Yahya Khan and Awani League Chief Sheikh Mujibur Rehman to augment already formidable force of 60,000 troops concentrated in the three cantonments of Dacca, Comilla and Jessore. At Chittagong thousands of East Bengalis had tried to prevent army from unloading their arms and the dockers refused to unload the ships)[39]

The objectives of the military dictator, having been achieved, the negotiations abruptly came to a crushing halt on the March 25, President General Yahya Khan returned to Karachi on March 26, followed by Bhutto the next day.[40]

Shortly after the President had flown to Karachi, the West Pakistan Army systematically moved to crush the citizen's administration which was set up by Sheikh Mujibur Rehman on March 1, 1971 and was since working effectively.[41] (One of the selected targets for extinction by the West Pakistani authorities had been the youth and the intellectuals of East Bengal. They opened fire at Dacca University killing hundreds of students, professors and scholars. Many girl students, residing in the University campus, were kidnapped and raped by the army. Later, on April 13, the Pakistani Troops forced 300 students of St. Francis Xavier School in Jessore to line up and machine gunned them. The parish Priest, an Italian, of Jessore town, was among the victims).[42]

While the President was still in Dacca a day before his departure, the Pakistani Army had machine gunned hundreds of innocent civilians at Chittagonng in an attempt to break through the barricades put up by the dock workers, who had earlier walked out and refused to handle the army supplies in keeping with the directives issued by the Awami Leader, Sheikh Mujibur Rehman. Subsequently, with the renewal of a reign of terror by the West Pakistani troops the situation in East Bengal once again became very tense and critical events followed in quick succession.[43].

Sheikh Mujibur Rehman declared a sovereign Independent Peoples' Republic of Bangladesh on March 26, 1971.[44]

General Yahya Khan despatched military units to launch a major attack and restore fully the authority of his Government in the turbulent Eastern Wing and consequently Martial Law was clamped down.

Amidst such a grave situation the free Bengal Radio announced on March 28, 1971 the formation of a provisional Bangladesh Government headed by the liberation army chief Major Zia Khan. Major Zia Khan was the Chief of the Liberation Army of Bangladesh since the resistance movement started on March 25, 1971.

He announced in a broadcast. "I hereby assume the powers of the Provisional Head of the Liberation Army of Swadhin Bangladesh. I order the freedom fighters of Bangladesh to continue the struggle till ultimate victory".[45] He appealed to the Government of peace loving countries to recognize the provisional Government and offer material assistance to the freedom fighters.

The Swadhin Bangladesh Kendra reported on March 29 that the Pakistani army, air force and navy had massacred 3,00,000 people, and it urged free nations of the world to come forward to check this genocide. It was reported that the people of Bangladesh were fighting a war against injustice and exploitation and for human rights and liberties. It appealed to India and Sri Lanka to help the freedom fighters in the interest of the "Survival of humanity and democracy endangered by the brutal invaders".[46]

In his broadcast Major Zia Khan said: "I, Major Zia Khan, provisional Commander-in-Chief of the Bangladesh army, hereby proclaimed on behalf of Sheikh Mujibur Rehman, the Independence of Bangladesh. I also declare that we have already formed a sovereign, legal government under Sheikh Mujibur Rehman which pledges to function as per law and the Constitution. We, therefore, appeal to all democratic and peace loving countries of the world to recognize the democratic Government of Bangladesh"[47].

In the month of December 1971, Sheikh Mujibur Rehman was arrested and taken to Karachi.[48]

After two months he was sent by General Tikka Khan to an unknown destination. After a month, press reports from London said that Sheikh Mujibur Rehman was in London.[49]

The people of East Bengal unitedly rose under the leadership of Sheikh Mujibur Rehman in protest against this arbitrary act of the President. Historic non-cooperation movement was started by Awami League. West Pakistani army units moved into suppress the movement martial law was imposed and many peaceful demonstrators were shot dead. School, College and the Universities were closed down. When East Pakistanis revolted against its own West Pakistani Government, India had to intervene and fought "14 day" war in December of 1971.[50] from March 26, 1971, onwards thousands of refugees began to cross over to take shelter into different parts of India. Roughly, eight and a half million refugees flooded into India.[51] Garo Hills of Meghalaya became one of the battle fronts of the war and gateway of refugees. Thousands and thousands were accommodated in Garo Hills. Every day hundreds and thousands of Refugees flooded into Garo Hills from 26 March, 1971 till December 1971, the highest number was recorded in the Government records was 2,82,947 on 9th December, 1971. During that period the refugees were not only from minority communities but also from the Muslims some were repatriated when the country returned to normal.

The East-West war ended in the month of December 1971. East Pakistan became an independent entity named Bangladesh, on the 16th December 1971.[52] Bangladesh was liberated with the help of mighty Indian army. The leader of this independence movement, Sheikh Mujibur Rehman came back to Bangladesh in the month of March 1972,[53] and became its first Prime Minister.[54]

After the first ever general election held on December 7, 1970, for the National Assembly, which was based on adult franchise, the leader of the majority party Sheikh Mujibur Rehman would have to be called upon to become the Prime Minister and form a representative government. However this did not happen, popular hopes were belied. The first meeting of the National Assembly scheduled for March 3, 1971, was postponed sine die by the President.

References

1. Vide the Assam Tribune Vol. 65 No. 48, Guahati, February 19, 2003.
2. Vide No. GRRO 7/65/3396 dated Dalu, the 20th March, 1965.
3. Bikash Marak Rechil Tura Te-tengkol, West Garo Hills on 30-12-2001.
4. Marak A. Grohonsing, *The Bangladesh and The Background* Unpublished document p. 2.
5. Amarendra. S. Sangma, *Bonepa A-tilla, Tura* on 29-12-2001.
6. Dinesh Chandra Sangma, *Tura Matehakol*, Tina, on 30-12-2001.

7. Ananta Sangma, *Tura*, on 30-12-2001.
8. Monoronjon Sangma, *Gimegre*, West Garo Hills, on 27-01-2002
9. Horesh Mankin Sangma. and Smt Bosilla Dajel Marak, Rongkongre, *WestGaro Hills*. on 28-01-2002.
10. Noho Rechil Marak and his wife Smt. Beronika Mankin Sangma, Rongkongre, *West Garo Hills*, 29-01-2002.
11. Jotindra Manda, Batabari Chirakawa, *West Garo Hills*, on 29-01-2002
12. Sotindra Chisim, Singwilgre, *West Garo Hills*, on 29-01-2002.
13. Mina Kuniar Rechil, Williainpur, *West Garo Hills*, on 30-01-2002.
14. L.D. Dewansing, S. Rongmuthu, D.V.S. Publishers, Guwahati, 1999, pp. 99-100.
15. *Ibid.*, p. 99.
16. *Ibid.*, 105.
17. *Ibid.*, pp. 105-06.
18. *Ibid.*, p. 106.
19. *Ibid.*
20. *Ibid.*, p. 108.
21. *Ibid.*, p. 134.
22. *Ibid.*, p. 152.
23. Malayalam Manorama, *Manorama Year Book*, 2002, 37th Ed., p. 265.
24. Ananta Sangma, *New Tura*, on 33rd 2001.
25. In the Constitution of 1962, Ayub Khan proclaimed a Presidential system.
26. Muhammad Ayub Khan, Who seized power in a coup in October 1958.
27. Marak Gronhonsing A., *The Bangladesh and the Background*, unpublished document, p. 1.
28. *Ibid.*, p. l.
29. *Ibid.*, p. 2.

30. *Ibid.*, pp. 2-3
31. Pakistan was proclaimed on Islamic Republic on March 1956.
32. Marak Grohonsing A., *The Bangladesh and the Backround,* Unpublished document, p. 3.
33. *Ibid.*, p. 4.
34. *Ibid.*
35. *Ibid.*
36. *Ibid.*, p. 5.
37. *Ibid.*
38. *Ibid.*
39. *Ibid.*
40. *Ibid.*, p. 6.
41. *Ibid.*
42. *Ibid.*
43. *Ibid.*, p. 7.
44. Malayala Manorama, *Manorama Year Book* 2002, 37th Ed. p. 323.
45. Marak Grohonsing A., *The Bangladesh and The Background,* Unpublished document, p. 7.
46. *Ibid.*, p. 7.
47. *Ibid.*, pp. 7-8.
48. *Ibid.*, p. 8.
49. *Ibid.*, p. 8.
50. Marak Grohonsing A., *The Bangladesh and The Background* Unpublished document, p. 10.
51. *Ibid.*
52. Malayala Manorama, *Manorama Year Book* 2002, 37th Ed, p. 266.
53. Marak Grohonsing A., *The Bangladesh and The Background,* Unpublished document, p. 8.
54. Malayala Manorama, *Manorama Year Book* 2002, Ed., p. 266.

Chapter IV

The Rehabilitation and Reclamation

This chapter deals with the rehabilitation and reclamation of the displaced persons of erstwhile East Pakistan during 1960s in the then Garo Hills district of Assam.

One of the records available from the Garo Hills District council (vide memorandum in respect of relief and rehabilitation of 1964 Refugees in Garo Hills, Dated, 18-05-1977) shows that due to the great turmoil described in the following pages in East Pakistan hundreds and thousands of distressed refugees crossed the international Indo-Pakistan border with harrowing tales of remorseless persecution and atrocities in 1964 and took refugee in Garo Hills.

Out of compassionate and humanitarian ground under the active leadership of Captain Williamson A. Sangma the then Chief Executive Member extended their hands to the government to cope with the grave situation. The District Council provided land, forest materials to construct camps at different places. And allowed their school buildings and market places for accommodation.

It was stated by Grohonshing A. Marak that towards the end of 1964 more than ten thousand non-tribal refugees returned to East Pakistan, but more than 75,000 Garo refugees still remained in Garo Hills. The second stage of this problem was the task of rehabilitation for those who stayed back. On the request of the Government of India the Garo Hills District council agreed to give settlement in the plain Mouzas of Garo Hills, provided unoccupied land was available. Grohonsing A. Marak himself was one of those involved in search of the unoccupied land.

Government of India sanctioned a scheme for reclamation of land for East Pakistani displaced persons in Garo Hills to be implemented by the Soil Conservation Department. The scheme which had been sanctioned by the Central Government was executed on the basis of equal benefit or fifty-fifty between the evacuees and the local people, otherwise to get the land from Ac "Nokma A'king" was very difficult without giving same benefit to the local people; because they also demanded the Government grant for reclamation of their land if they give their land to the refugees. The first scheme was implemented and inaugurated at A-karok Songgiital (Mendal) 40 miles away from Tura, which was on the Tura-Bajengdpba-Paikan road. The inaugural function took place on Friday November 6, 1964. On that day for the first batch of 24 refugee families from Ganol Relief Camp, reclaimed lands were bonded over by late Capt W. A. Sangma Chief Executive Member, Garo Hills restrict Council.

Since Garo Hills District Council is a Constitutional body with authority over land in the District, despite non-availability of suitable lands, they undertook the responsibility of rehabilitating migrants from East Pakistan.

The amount received by the Garo Hills District Council from the Government between 1964 and 1968 was Rs. 42,71,226/- (Forty two lakhs seventy one thousands two hundred and twenty six only); out of which Rs. 25,98,726/- was given as loan and Rs. 16,72,500/- as grant. The amount shown above had been sanctioned under different schemes towards relief and rehabilitation works. Different categories of migrant families were rehabilitated under different Schemes as per Table 4.1.

Table 4.I

Sl. No.	*Name of Schemes*	*Agri. Families*	*Business families*	*Employees families*	*Total*	*Remarks*
1.	Khas Land of Scheme of 1,500 Agri. Migrant families	1,011	—	—	1,011	—
2.	Non-Agri. Scheme of 150 Non-Agri. Migrant Families	—	135	34	169'	Employee families are paid only single Housing loan
3.	Soil Conservation Scheme of 500 Agriculture Migrant families	500	—	—	500	All are agri. familites
4.	Soil Conservation Scheme of 1,000 Agriculture Migrant families	409	—	—	409	— do —
	Total	**1320**	**135**	**34**	**2089**	

Table 4.2 shows the area of land reclaimed and allotted to the migrant families and number of migrant families settled under the Khas Land Scheme for the rehabilitation of 1,500 Agricultural migrant families in Garo Hills District Council.

Table 4.2

Sl. No	*Rehabilitation sites*	*Total No. of families settled.*	*Area of Land Reclaimed and allotted*			*No. of fully settled*	*No. of families not fully settled*
			B	K	L		
1.	Misikona	16	105-	1-	11	15	1
2.	Jamanggiri	8	29	-0-	8	6	2
3.	Bongpara	7		Nil		Nil	7
4.	Rerapara	7	42	-0	00	7	Nil
5.	Batabari	43	180	-0	00	43	Nil
6.	Jenggrip	55		Nil		Nil	55
7.	Upper Kamari	21	131	-1	16	21	Nil
8.	Goramara	12	56	-0	00	9	3
9.	Modupara	12	34	-1	00	1	11
10.	Kalazar	28	76	-4	06	6	22
11.	Rangatari	18	66	-0	00	9	9
12.	Gandhipara	38	129	02	11	15	23
13.	Gomaijora	43	63	03	15	1	42
14.	Sonamite	15	43	0	00	2	13
15.	Dewsali	25	48	03	11	3	22
16.	Wankola Dakop	45	52	01	10	Nil	45
17.	Asugiri	1		Nil		Nil	1
18.	Dalu Kujikura	1		Nil		Nil	1
19.	Dopatchigiri	3		Nil		Nil	3
20.	Morapara	2		Nil		Nil	2
21.	Bajugiri	1		Nil		Nil	1
22.	Dingkhajora	2		Nil		Nil	2
23.	Baburampara	1		Nil		Nil	1
24.	Adang Chandobhoi	6		Nil		Nil	6

(*Contd.*)

(*Contd.*)

Sl. No	Rehabilitation sites	Total No. of families settled.	Area of Land Reclaimed and allotted B	K	L	No. of fully settled	No. of families not fully settled
25.	Dalugaon	1		Nil		Nil	1
26.	Thibapara	2		Nil		Nil	2
27.	Gangbanga	1		Nil		Nil	1
28.	Sangbanggiri	35	44	00	15	Nil	35
29.	Singira	30	180	00	00	3	27
30.	Balapara	5		Nil		Nil	5
31.	Boldampitbari	46	90	00	08	3	43
32.	Khasbil	46	50	04	08	Nil	46
33.	Salbilla	39	186	00	00	39	Nil
34.	Balujora	40	48	04	12	Nil	40
35.	Chapati	8		Nil		Nil	8
36.	Ronggekgiri	1		Nil		Nil	1
37.	Kalaichar	100	478	02	11	83	17
38.	Sampalgiri	14	120	00	00	14	Nil
39.	Kotchugiri	1		Nil		Nil	20
40.	Galwanggiri	1		Nil		Nil	1
41.	Jongkol	1		Nil		Nil	1
42.	Neldkona	25		Nil		Nil	25
43.	Nidanpur (Tikrikilla)	204	1206	00	00	204	Nil
	Total	**1029**	**3438**	**03**	**15**	**484**	**545**

It was stated that in some of the rehabilitation sites that the area of Land Reclaimed and allotted to the migrant families has still to be verified and as such the area of Land actually reclaimed and allotted to the migrant families may be more or less that of the total area of land as shown in this Table.

Table 4.3 shows the area of land reclaimed and allotted to the migrant families and number of migrant families settled under the soil Conservation Scheme for the rehabilitation of 1,000 Agriculturist migrant families in Garo Hills.

Table 4.3

Sl. No.	*Name of Rehabilitation sites*	*Total No. of families settled.*	*Area of Land Reclaimed and allotted to the migrants but yet to be formally settled.*			*No. of Families fully settled*	*No. of families not fully settled.*
			B	K	L		
1.	Bolkinggre	30	117	01	11	29	1
2.	Simpalgre	25	129	01	11	16	9
3.	Chisimgre	20	114	00	06	17	3
4.	A'karok Songgittal	3	18	03	18	3	Nill
5.	Sasatgre Part (I)	63	317	00	00	44	19
6.	Sasatgre Part (II)	25	148	00	09	25	Nill
7.	Nengmandalgre	20	102	04	02	16	4
8.	Bolbokgre Part (I)	6	29	01	05	5	1
9.	Bolbokgre Part (II)	5	21	01	00	4	1
10.	Bolbokgre Part (III)	7	23	03	03	2	5
11.	Bolbokgre Part (IV)	5	17	01	01	1	4
12.	Bolbokgre Part (V)	10	35	03	07	2	8
13.	Jeldopara	14	88	00	13	14	Nill
14.	Watregre	13	108	02	13	15	10
15.	Chibragre	13	77	02	16	11	2
16.	Allagre	5)	48	01	11	4	1
17.	Jetra A-du	10	60	00	14	10	Nill
18.	A-karok Songgital	10	58	02	11	10	Nill
19.	Kaikuri (Kotchugre)	33	231	01	14	30	3
20.	Chikasingre	6	36	02	02	6	Nill
21.	Mangmpara	10		Nill		Nill	10
	Total	**345**	**1843**	**01**	**03**	**264**	**81**

Whether the area of land actually reclaimed and allotted to them is exactly as shown in the table has not been verified.

Table 4.4 shows the area of land reclaimed and allotted to the migrant families and number of migrant families settled under the Soil Conservation Scheme for the rehabilitation of 500 Agriculturist migrant families in Garo Hills.

Table 4.4

Sl. No.	Name of Rehabilitation sites	Total No. of families settled.	Area of Land Reclaimed and allotted to the migrants but yet to be formally settled.			No. of families folly settled	No. of families not fully settled.
			B	K	L		
1.	Bolonggre	14	40	0	19	3	11
2.	Gokolgre Part (I)	25	81	03	03	3	22
3.	GokolgrePart (II)	25	96	04	03	13	12
4.	Remgre	11	39	03	00	2	9
5.	Mendal	16	87	04	17	10	6
6.	Jigabari area	182	1155	01	00	164	18
7.	Dingrapara	15	79	03	10	12	3
8.	Chandrapafhar	30	141	00	03	19	11
9.	Chokchokia	19	104	00	01	4	10
10.	Ronggopgre	30	119	04	11	15	15
11.	Balachanda	87	459	04	12	68	19
	Total	**454**	**2407**	**3**	**07**	**324**	**130**

In these rehabilitation sites the area of land reclaimed and allotted to the migrant families is yet to be verified.

The above three tables show that there are 75 numbers of rehabilitation sites but only in 54 numbers of rehabilitated sites migrant families have been rehabilitated. In the other 21 rehabilitation sites there were no lands reclaimed and allotted to the migrants. Out of 1,828 families, fully settled families are 1,072 and not fully settled families are 756.

The area of land reclaimed and allotted to the migrant families is reported to be 7,689 bighas 3 kattas and 5 lesas; but it is still subject to proper survey. These are all agricultural migrant families, rehabilitated under different schemes in the year 1966-68.

Besides thirty eight new Garo migrant families, since categorized as Small Trader families were finally resettled during 1973-74 with the following rehabilitation benefits.

1. Business Loan	Rs. 1,21,600/-[3]
2. Housing Loan	Rs. 55,100/-
3. Maintenance Grant	Rs. 31.730/-[4]

One hundred sixty two new Garo migrant families were finally resettled in Small Trader Scheme during 1974-75, with the following benefits.

1. Business Loan	Rs. 4,05,000/-
	Rs. 81,000/-
2. Housing Loan	Rs. 2,02,500/-
	Rs. 32,400/-
3. Maintenance Grant	Rs. 39,804/-

Twelve Garo permanent liability families were resettled as small traders during 1975-76 with the following benefits

1. Business Loan	Rs. 38,000/-
2. Housing Loan	Rs. 15,000/-
3. Maintenance Grant	Rs. 2,235/-

Two hundred fifty three Garo families were sent to various rehabilitation sites in Garo Hills District in 1966-68, but due to the non-availability of cultivable land the families could not be allotted full quota of land. To enable the families to resettle themselves, they were re-categorised as small traders by the state government and the proposed scheme was accordingly submitted to the Government of India. Since Government of India did not agree to the proposal, the scheme was treated as finally closed[5]

One hundred fourteen Garo families were resettled in Tikrikifla area in the Garo Hills District by the composite state of Assam during 1966, but in 1970, the cultivable land provided by the Garo Hills District council and allotted to the families were taken back by the local people through a court decree. The families became landless again. There after the Government of Assam sanctioned a lump sum grant of Rs. 2,000/- only for the needy families for their immediate relief

During 1973, the Deputy Commissioner Garo Hills revived the case and submitted necessary proposal for final resettlement of these families while the scheme was under examination by the state Government, the Deputy Commissioner, Garo Hills advised the State Government to keep the scheme in abeyance as negotiations with the Garo Hills District Council to provide land for the families was being initiated. Subsequently in January, 1976 the Deputy Commissioner, Garo Hills again intimated that the Garo Hills District was not in a position to allot cultivate land and submitted a revised scheme for grant of Rs. 3,000/ - as loan to each family to enable the 114 families to arrange cultivable land for themselves and to finally resettle themselves[6]

It was learnt that before initiating Rehabilitation measures an agreement was signed between the Deputy

Commissioner and the Chief Executive Member, Garo Hills District Council, Tura on 22-02-66[7].

According to the agreement the Garo Hills District Council, Tura, implemented a Khas Land scheme of 1,500 agriculturist families out of which only 1,011 families were rehabilitated in different parts of Garo Hills District. Under the aforementioned scheme, two batches of refugee families of 253 and 114 families were rehabilitated in the year 1967 and 1968 respectively. They were provided with homestead plots, housing loan and bullock loan only and they did not get full quota of cultivable land so they requested the state Government to re-categorize the families as small traders families and to provide them business loan. But it did not materialize since Government of Meghalaya treated the scheme as finally closed.[8]

When no agriculture or cultivable land was allotted to 253 migrant families, since they had came out from the camp in July, 1966, they were paid cash dole upto November, 1968 for continuation of their livelihood.

It was found by the researchers that every migrant refugee should have been registered as a citizen of India under the provisions of section (5)(I)(a)/(d) of the Citizenship Act, 1955, while they were in the relief camp. Those who had citizenship certificates were only rehabilitated in the Garo Hills District during 1960s. The same opportunity was not given to the Bangladesh evacuees during Bangladesh Liberation war in 1971 as Government of India cut off issuing citizenship certificate in that year.

Table 4.5 shows receipt, expenditure and balance under different schemes for R.R. etc. works under the Garo Hills District Council, as on 31-3-1977.

Table 4.5

Sl. No.	Name of Scheme	Reciept		Expenditure		Balance	
		Loan	Grant	Loan	Grant	Loan	Grant
		Rs. P.	Rs. P.	Rs. P.	Rs. P.	Rs. P.	Rs. P.
1.	Khas Land Scheme for rehabilitation of 150 migrant families	14,36,00/-	1,00,00/-	12,64,997.39	5,16,399.04	1,71,00.61	416899.04(-)
2.	Non-Agriculture Scheme of 150 Non-Agriculture families	225,00/-	22,500	2,18,500.00	20,100.00	6,500.00	2400.00
3.	Under the soil convervation Scheme of 500 Agriculture families.	4,24,726/-	—	3,59,736.25	—	64.939.75	—
4.	Under the soil conservation Scheme of 1000 Agriculture families	5,13,000/-	—	1,71,935.00	—	3,41,065.00	—
5.	Grant for supply of bullocks to local Tribal families	—	5,00,000/-	—	4,93,440.00	—	9,11,462.35
6.	Grant for land reclaimation & Irrigation to local Triball families	—	10,50,000/-	—	1,38,537.65	—	
	Grant Total	**25,98,726/-**	**16,72,500/-**	**20,15,168.64**	**11,73,976.69**	**5,83,55.36**	**4,98,523.31**

Expenditure Incurred by the Council in 1964

1. Khas Land Scheme 1,500 families Rehabilitated 1,029 Agriculture families.
   (i) House Loan @ 500/- per family paid for 1,029 families.
   Rs. 5,20,953,49 Bond signed all.
   (ii) Bullock Loan @ 415/-per family.

For 178 families	73,870.00	
For 410@ 425/-	1,47,250.00	Bond not signed.
For 389 @ 435/-	1,69,215.00	
977 families	4,17,335.00	

   (iii) Seed Loan @ 50/- per family for 540 families.
   Rs. 27,000/- Bond signed.
2. Khas Land Scheme 150 Non-Agriculture families.
   (i) House Loan @ 500/- per family... for 169 families = Rs. 84500/-
   (ii) Business Loan @ 1,000/- per family = Rs. 135000/-
3. Soil Conservation 1,000 Agriculture families.
   (i) Bullock for 15 families @ 415/-... = Rs. 6225/-
   Bullock for 307 families @ 425/-... = Rs. 1,30,475/-
   Bullock for 81 families @ 435/-... = Rs. 35235/-
   = Rs.1,71,935/-
   Bond not signed.
4. Soil Conservation 500 families.
   Bullock for 500 families = Rs. 2,37,500.00
   Bond not signed.
   Half Cash dole for 494 families @ different rate = Rs. 84,736.25
   Bond Signed
   = Rs. 3,22,236.25
   Total = Rs. 16,78,959.75 P.

List of Rehabilitation Centre of Migrant families Under East Garo Hills is given in Table 4.6.

List of Rehabilitation Centre of Migrant families Under West Garo Hills is given in Table 4.7.

Tabte. 4.6

Sl. No.	Name of Village	Mouza No.	No. of families	Home stead Land			Cultivable Land			Total		
				B	K	L	B	K	L	B	K	L
1.	Dingripara	III	15	18	03	15	60	04	2	79	2	17
2.	Mendal	III	16	20	0	00	80	1	5	100	–1	5
3.	Gokulgre Ist & 2nd	III	59	56	4	5	250	4	8	307	–3	13
4.	A.karok Songgital & Songitcham	III	13	16	–1	10	78	1	10	94	3	0
5.	Chisim A.dinggre	III	20	25	1	10	160	4	77	186	1	7
6.	Remgre	III	11	15	4	10	66	2	10	82	2	0
7.	Ronggopgre	III	39	36	1	5	180	0	0	216	1	5
8.	Watregre	III	25	30	1	10	145	1	5	175	2	15
9.	Sasatgre (Chiokgre Ist and 2nd)	IV	88	101	2	10	332	2	10	434	0	0
10.	Bolldnggre	IV	30	36	0	0	120	4	12	158	4	12
11.	Nengmandalgre	IV	20	25	1	10	90	1	13	115	3	3
12.	Jetragre	IV	10	15	1	15	60	3	5	76	0	0
	'B' Total		**328**	**379**	**4**	**–0**	**1627**	**–1**	**–17**	**2025**	**0**	**17**

Table 4.7

Sl. No.	Name of Village	Mouza No.	No. of families.	Home stead Land			Cultivable Land			Total		
				B	K	L	B	K	L	B	K	L
1.	Khamari	V	21	24	4	10	84	03	5	109	2	15
2.	Singra	V	29	32	01	15	116	2	5	148	-4	0
3.	Sabanggre	V	35	40	2	10	105	3	10	146	1	0
4.	Jengrip	V	53	60	4	10	212	4	5	273	3	15
5.	Kalajhar	V	26	30	3	15	130	1	18	161	0	13
6.	Wankola Dakop	V	44	48	2	05	176	4	10	225	1	15
7.	Deosali	V	25	30	1	15	100	3	12	131	0	7
8.	Boldampitbari	V	37	40	2	5	111	4	10	152	1	15
9.	Nidanpur	VI	201	210	5	5	1206	0	00	1416	4	5
10.	Gmnaijhora	Vi	39	40	4	10	117	4	2	158	3	12
11.	Balujhora	VI	13	20	1	15	40	2	3	60	30	18
	Koikuri (Kotchugre)	VII	33	37	1	10	99	4	16	137	1	6
13.	Batabari I & II	VII	40	45	4	10	102	3	14	138	3	4
14.	Jigabari Centre											
15.	Chokcholda											
16.	Balachanda	VII	318	350	4	10	1590	4	5	1941	3	15
17.	Chandrapafhar											
18.	Habima Simulgre											
19.	Jeldopara (Mangmgre)	VII	10	15	0	0	60	0	00	75	0	0

(Contd.)

(*Contd.*)

Sl. No.	Name of Village	Mouza No.	No. of families.	Home stead Land			Cultivable Land			Total		
				B	K	L	B	K	L	B	K	L
20.	Salbilla	VII	31	35	4	10	124	2	10	160	2	0
21.	Saitipalgre	VII	20	25	4	5	100	3	12	126	2	17
22.	Khasb l (Monabari)	VII	40	46	2	10	90	4	18	137	2	8
23.	Kalaichor	VIII	100	105	3	15	600	0	0	705	3	15
24.	Rerapara	X	6	9	0	0	30	3	15	39	3	15
25.	Jamanggre	x	6	8	2	10	30	4	5	39	1	15
26.	Bongpara	X	7	9	3	10	42	0	0	51	3	10
27.	Misikona	x	16	18	2	10	65	0	0	83	2	10
28.	Gorainara	x	12	15	0	0	60	4	0	75	4	0
29.	Modupara	x	11		3	10	36	1	14	46	0	4
30.	Ranggatari	x	15	42	4	10	45	2	10	63	1	15
31.	Gandhipara	x	39	42	4	10	166	4	5	7209	3	15
		"A"	**1227**	**1375**	**0**	**0**	**5651**	**3**	**4**	**7026**	**3**	**4**
		B"	**328**	**0**	**0**	**0**	**1627**	**1**	**17**	**2025**	**0**	**17**
	Grand Total		**1555**	**1772**	**4**	**0**	**7279**	**0**	**1**	**9051**	**4**	**1**

List of villages and area of Land allotted to the displaced persons of East Pakistani with P.P. and Dag. Nos. is given in Table 4.8.

Table 4.8

Sl. No.	*Name of Villages*	*No. of Patta*	*No of Dag*	*Area of Land*		
				B	K	L
1.	Jigabari	1	1	5	1	8
2.	Balujhora	1	3	13	3	6
3.	Batabari	1	1	15	0	0
4.	Modupara	1	1	1	2	0
5.	Rangatani	1	3	4	3	01
6.	Balachanda	1	2	8	3	10
7.	Balapara	1	1	7	0	6
8.	Jenggrip (I)	1	2	3	2	0
9.	Kalaigao	1	2	6	4	14
10.	Khasbil (Monabari)	2	6	14	3	2
11.	Bagadol	1	1	2	0	0
12.	Balughat	3	4	9	0	9
13.	Goramara	5	15	48	1	5
14.	1st Dakop	3	6	21	0	13
15.	Upper Kalaichor	7	8	27	4	15
16.	Balachanda (Namabila)	10	14	31	1	10
17.	Kotchugre (Koikuri)	4	10	42	3	8
18.	Habima Smgwilgre	8	13	42	3	7
19.	Kalazar	2	2	11	3	18
20.	Misikona	1	4	10	3	0
21.	Salbma	4	8	19	0	17
22.	Sampalgre	60	128	238	4	2
23.	Nagorgao	1	8	29	1	13
24.	Williampur (Nidanpur)	2	4	5	2	3
25.	Boldampitbari	3	5	9	0	5
26.	2ndDakop	2	7	30	3	19
27.	Lower Kalaichor	5	11	28	1	9

(*Contd.*)

(*Contd.*)

Sl. No.	Name of Villages	No. of Patta	No of Dag	Area of Land B	K	L
28.	K.ftrnein	8	14	81	2	3
29.	Mangrugre (Silkota)	5	10	81	4	6
30.	1st Wakantagre	10	18	111	3	5
31.	2nd Wakantagre	2	5	24	3	12
32.	Chokchokia	17	37	165	4	14
33.	Deosali	8	18	33	3	6
34.	Panbari	47	76	109	3	12
35.	Gumaijhora	28	114	104	3	18
36.	Nidanpur	8	18	88	3	17
	Grand Total	**265**	**579**	**1491**	**2**	**10**

One of the records available shows that the new migrant families of former East Pakistan (families who arrived from 1.1.64 to 25.3.71) were rehabilitated in the States outside Dandakaranya and West Bengals indicated in Table 4.9.

Table 4.9

	State	Agriculture	Small Trade	Total
1.	Andhra Pradesh	1786	135	1921
2.	Assam	6784	8714	15498
3.	Bihar	1032	1552	2584
4.	Karnataka	723	—	723
5.	Madhya Pradesh	5305	2002	7307
6.	Maharashtra	5674	509	6183
7.	Manipur	145	—	145
8.	Meghalaya	1938	212	2150
9.	Orissa	6	253	259
10.	Punjab		3	3
11.	Tripura	5675	707	6382
12.	Uttar Pradesh	1823	601	2424
13.	Arunachal Pradesh	2902	—	2902
14.	Rajasthan	573	335	908
15.	Andamans	774	31	805
	Total	**35,140**	**15,054**	**50,194**

The above statistics show that in Meghalaya State 2,150 migrant families were rehabilitated. Out of which 2,089 families were rehabilitated in Garo Hills District of Meghalaya.

Repatriation in 1971

Before 1971 those who crossed the border to take shelter in India they were given a citizenship certificate by the Government of India. Many East Pakistani displaced persons were rehabilitated in different parts of India. But in 1971 Bangladesh Liberation War those who crossed the border to take shelter in Indian Territory same facility was not given to them by the Government.

In 1971, those who came to Assam and Meghalaya due to political unrest in East Bengal they were to get themselves registered, as per the order issued by the Government of India under Foreigners Registration Act, 1946.

All such refugees were to have a valid Registration Card in their possession issued by the Registration authority in which their place and the period permitted to them to stay was also mentioned. Registration certificate were issued to the evacuees by the Police Officer.

The state Government fixed the first December, 1971 as the last date by which the refugees were to complete registration work including endorsement on certificate regarding the period of validity. All new comers were required to register themselves within 24 hours of entering into India. If any one violated the decision mentioned above, appropriate action by the Government was taken.

During 1971 influx the Government of India and the State Government of Assam promulgated an order under the Foreigners Act of 1946, where evacuees of East Pakistan had been given temporary permission to stay in the adjourning areas of the Indian Union. After East and West Pakistan civil war was over on December 16, 1971 and the situation was restored to normal circumstances the Government of India and the Government of Bangladesh jointly ordered them to move back to their respective places (i.e. to Bangladesh).

Thousands and thousands of refugees from East Bengal who had taken shelter in India since 26-03-1971, due to political unrest between East and West Pakistan which ended after 14 days war in December and East got victory over West Pakistan on December 16, 1971, there after those evacuees were repatriated to their own places.

The number of evacuees returning to Bangladesh from Garo Hills District since last fortnight of December, 1971 upto the 29 January 1972 has been given in Table 4.10.

Table 4.10

Sl. No.	*Name of Refugees Camps*	*Non-Muslim*	*Muslim*	*Christian*	*Others*	*Total*
1.	Baghmara	43,007	3,036	14,703	6,789	67,535
2.	Sibbari	22,451	5,805	4,794	–	33,050
3.	Dunmikura	2,815	2,758	5509	–	11,082
4.	Minene	875	1,587	4340	–	6,,802
5.	Machangpani	3778	22	1157	–	4,957
6.	Dimapara	3620	90	7220	480	11,410
7.	Data (Vety. Camp.)	2,593	2739	3811	–	9143
8.	Chandabhoi	6,752	631	911	–	8294
9.	Sisengpara	1533	635	1,343	–	3,511
10.	Purakhasia	3,794	2559	1,592	–	7945
11.	Halchati	630	218	212	–	1060
12.	Mahendraganj (Patijhora & Kalaipara)	8462	8335	457	1240	18494
13.	Ampati	2481	0,505	55	382	12,423
14.	Chibinang	755	5	5	–	765
	From other places staying with friends and relatives	6477	902	9287	–	16,666
	Total	**1,10,223**	**38,927**	**55,081**	**8891**	**2,13,122**

Vide Memo. No. DSB (P)/T/50/72/526 dated Tura. 1st February, 1972.

Thana wise Figure of Evacuees returned to Bangladesh under different Police Station upto 29-01-1972 from Garo Hills District is given in Table 4.11.

Table 4.11

	Police Station	*No. of Evacuees*
1.	Begamganj	2,125
2.	Basail	1033
3.	Belkuchi	3267
4.	Dewanganj	5268
5.	Dhannai	226
6.	Fulsari,	1527
7.	Gaibanda	1462
8.	Islampur	11,274
9.	Jamalpur	15,142
10.	Ghatail	4860
11.	Nunia	502
12.	Modon	1360
13.	Sribardi	14,400
14.	Serpur	10,765
15.	Sripur	5903
16.	Sirajganj	1425
17.	Sahaduliapara	305
18.	Phulpuri	7142
19.	Purbhadala	6691
20.	Haluaghat	14,887
21.	Mymensing	47,162
22.	Iswarganj	1401
23.	Netrokona	11,461
24.	Byhata	235
25.	Kalmakandha	1326
26.	Atpara	205

(Contd.)

Bangladeshi Immigrants in Meghalaya

(*Contd.*)

	Police Station	No. of Evacuees
27.	Gauripur	702
28.	Tarail	917
29.	Lokhai	706
30.	Karimganj	13
31.	Tangail	12,345
32.	Gafargaon	922
33.	Naltabari	286
34.	Tripura	12
35.	Roughpur	1124
36.	Kaliakandi	130
37.	Chihnan	302
38.	Lalbag	112
39.	Kaliganj	212
40.	Kungrani	110
41.	Lalmanihat	516
42.	Mdhupur	1306
43.	Sanghata	205
44.	Santuria	22
45.	Tozgaon	50
46.	Dacca	62
47.	Jassure	512
48.	Faridpur	614
49.	Conmulla	215
50.	Nokia	200
51.	Muktagaoha	1252
52.	Baksiganj	2873
53.	Kalihati	150
54.	Ramna	114
55.	Brahmanbaria	21
56.	Suhagpur	31

(*Contd.*)

(*Contd.*)

	Police Station	No. of Evacuees
57.	Nababganj	21
58.	Haripur	205
59.	Tarapura	150
60.	Atna	3202
61.	Rajbari	3
62.	Kandua	12
63.	Kishoreganj	1260
64.	Nandail	1931
65.	Durgapur	2302
66.	Dinajpura	6106
67.	Noakhali	21
68.	Pabna	10
	Total	**2,13,122**

Total number of evacuees entered between 26-03-1971 upto 9-12-1971.	=	2,82,947
Released under prior to introduction of registration under Foreigner Act.	=	12,696
Released on undertaking after registration under Foreigner Act.	=	41,798
Died in various diseases.	=	6,833
Joined in member family before registration	=	8498
Total Returned	=	2,13,122
Total	=	2,82,947

References

1. *See* Memo No. GSC. 28 (k)/3136-86. Dated Tura, the 2nd November, 1964.
2. *See* Govt. of India's letter No. 21 (26)/72-R.H. IV/RH. V. dated, 20-08-73.
3. No. G. 28-00-19 (15)/73 dated 18-05-75.

4. *See* Government of India letter No. 17 03V73-Rh.V, dated 30-11-73.
5. Vide Government of Meghalaya their letter No. MRR 34/75/131. Dated, Shillong, 30th July, 1976.
6. Government of Meghalaya Letter No. TRO-67/71-72/part/74 dated, Tura, 17th October, 1977.
7. Vide their letter No. MRR 19/72/342 dated 5-3-76.

Chapter V

The Impacts of the Cross Border Movement

Political Impact

The Garo Hills District Council was constituted in the year 1952. Late Captain Willliamson A. Sangma was the first Chief Executive Member of that council. Power was vested in the District Council under the sixth schedule of the Constitution of India to administer and legislate on the allotment, occupation, and use or settling the land[1].

Regarding the rehabilitation of the displaced persons of the former East Pakistan, Garo Hills District Council played an important role. For the resettlement of the Garo refugees in the Garo Hills District, an agreement was arrived at between Garo Hills District Council and the Government of Assam. Many schemes and grants, for rehabilitation of the refugees in Garo Hills Districts, were sanctioned by the Government of India to be implemented through Garo Hills District Council. On that basis they rehabilitated many Garo refugees along the plain Mouzas of the District.

The political scenario of Garo Hills underwent a tremendous change by the coming of the refugees from East Pakistan. Within the parameter of the Garo Hills politics, the impact of the Garo refugees on it was great. The prominent parties like Indian National Congress (INC), the Garo National Council (GNC), made the utmost use of the immigrants to win elections. In fact it became the solid vote bank in the general elections both of the Assam State Legislative Assembly and Meghalaya State Legislative Assembly.

The impact on the general elections was manifested in the general elections of 1967 and 1972, as well. Shrewd politicians like Capt. Williamson. A. Sangma made maximum use of the opportunity to get votes in the elections. With farsightedness he dispersed them in the plain zones like Garobadha, Jigabari, Singimari, Balachanda, Nidanpur, Tikrikilla and in certain pockets of Garo Hills. His aim was to reduce the Muslims of plains into minority, who supported the Congress party[2]. After rehabilitation of those displaced persons the Muslims become a minority in those areas.

Mina Kumar Rechil of Nidanpur (Williampur) was stated to have said that after their rehabilitation in 1966, while campaigning for 1967 General Election for the Assam Assembly Late Capt. W.A. Sangma passionately spoke to the immigrants that he and his party had rehabilitated them sympathetically and moreover extended much humanitarian assistance. In return they were asked to give their cooperation as well as their votes for his party i.e. All Party Hills Leaders' Conference (A.P.H.L.C). The displaced persons, who were rehabilitated by them, also became his faithful voters; this relationship continued for many years. Needless to mention that in the general elections of 1967, they voted for the A.P.H.L.C. All the Assembly seats of Garo Hills were swept by his party. There was an added appeal because during that period his party was leading the people in Hill State Movement.

The MLAs like Capt. Sangma, Modi. K. Marak, Grohonsingh. A. Marak and Bronson W. Momin worked hand in hand in order to achieve their political goal. After Meghalaya attained statehood in the first ever General Elections for the Meghalaya Legislative Assembly, held in 1972 A.P.H.L.C. secured a majority of 32 seats out of 60 seats[1]. It was a great success because it paved the way for him to become the first Chief Minister of newly created Meghalaya state.

The Communist Party of India (C.P.I.) also came into existence in Garo Hills and it was with the support and membership of the displaced persons who, while coming from East Pakistan, brought it along with them, although it did not became popular in Garo Hills. The indigenous people were unfamiliar with them. The veteran politicians like Lahit Sarkar and Robin Rema, who were associated members with experienced politicians like Mani Singh then communist leader in East Pakistan, organized the party in Garo Hills and could only penetrate into certain pockets of Garo Hills. Its impact was clearly evident from their participation in the General Election of 1967.[2]

The Muslims in plain zones were strong supporters of District Congress and this continued till the General

Election of 1967[3]. Other non-Garos living in plain belts tried to merge their political interest with those of the neighbouring plains as well as that of the outer hills of the District. Hajongs, Rabhas, Koches, Banais, Dalus and Bengalis predominantly tried to link with Indian National Congress. To defeat them Captain W.A. Sangma and Gronsingh A. Marak rehabilitated Garo Refugees in the plain mouzas. With their support in the Phulbhari constituency, where the Muslims cultivators predominated, the congress candidate Emonsing. M. Sangma was defeated by Bronson W. Momin, the A.P.H.L.C. candidate in the General election of 1967 for Assam Legislative Assembly.

Immediate Effect of the Influx

In 1971, refugee influx, school buildings and market places were also used for providing accommodation and relief work. Normal functioning of schools and markets were affected along the border areas. Not finding room enough for themselves in the temporary refugee camps constructed for the purpose or unwilling to stay in place at far distant from the borderline, thousands of refugees, many of whom were suffering from dreadful infectious diseases, such as leprosy, small-pox, measles etc.[1] forcibly trespassed into the homes, homesteads, gardens, *aus* and *jhum* fields etc. of Garo Hills. The refugees robbed fruits, roots and vegetables etc. and whatever else attracted them from '*jhum*' fields and private gardens.

The field's standing paddy and other crops, gardens and *jhum* fields on the hill slopes of Baghmara and neighbouring border villages were trodden down by thousands of refugees, causing incalculable economic ruin to the bonafide inhabitants.[2]

By their careless and thoughtless way of disposing of their dead at places close to human habitation, they sometimes dumped the corpses, almost half-exposing them. They passed stool any where, except latrines, with utter this regard for hygiene and sanitation, in this way thousands of refugees polluted the air and drinking water of the border villages. The stinking odour became absolutely intolerable all around, which posed serious health hazard which jeopardised which the people of the area. Many refugees suffering from cholera, dysentery and other infectious diseases died. It is also learnt from D.S. Rongmuthu's complaint letter that selling of jack-fruits, mangos, fresh fish, dry-fishs and pork at the Baghmara market was banned, which caused economic set-back to the indigenous people of the border villages. The local people living in those areas were emotionally and psychologically disturbed by all these events. Many of the refugees even started petty business in the villages and markets for their livelihood. On 19 January, 2002, it was told by Bilsing Ch. Marak of Danakgre, (son of Najing Sangma, Nokma of Danakgre A king), that on the roadside of New Tura and Najing bazaar, Tura, petty business establishments like tea stalls and vegetable shops were started by the refugees. Side by side with theme some local people also started small enterprises like refugees. Even in Williamnagar town, selling of various locally produced vegetables were initiated by them; the local people of the new township were not used to selling them. Those migrants, while in East Pakistan, used to speak Bengali fluently. On account of this they did not have language problem in running the business with non-Garo speaking people.

Before coming to Garo Hills some of them studied in Bengali medium schools up to standard X, F.A. and B.A. They knew the value of education. They urged their children to get education, since there was plenty of scopes for getting Government jobs in Garo Hills. Many of them continued their study after coming to Garo Hills. At present many of them are working in government offices as well as private institutions. Some of them became high ranking officers like magistrates, doctors, engineers, etc. Many of the Government jobs and in the private sectors are also occupied by them. There is a feeling that indigenous people of Garo Hills are being dominated by them.

The Garos of Garo Hills, wherever they are, practice matrilineal system, according to which the septs, clans and surnames are all derived from the line of motherhood. In the marriage system of the Garos of the Garo Hills, usually groom is brought to the bride's place and wedding ceremony takes place at girl's place. The immigrants from East Pakistan were influenced by Bengali culture. Some of them, who settled in Garo Hills, tried to continued their custom and system used in Bangladesh, in which girls were taken to boys, place for the wedding ceremony, in contravention of the indigenous customary laws.

Before coming of the East Pakistani refugees into Garo Hills, it was rare to hear about the stealing, looting, robbing and taking things from the *jhum* garden and other places from others; if the things were kept or scattered on the outside nobody used to take if any; only after they were rehabilitated in Garo Hills, looting, robbing and stealing was heard often. In every cash of stealing, robbing and looting their involvement was heard of. While talking about such type of happening it does not mean that all of them were bad, yet some of them were good people, too.

Impact on Environment

Due to refugee influx from East Pakistan there occurred reduction in forest areas in Garo Hills. During mass influx in 1964 and in 1971 the immediate problem that arose was providing shelter to thousands of refugees. The District Council provided land and forest materials to construct camps at different places, along the Indo-Bangladesh border in Garo Hills. Lots of valuable trees from 'Under State Forest' (U.S.F.) were indiscriminately exploited for construction of camps as well as for fire wood. Huge quantities of Sal and non Sal trees, bamboos were cut down for construction of houses while they were being rehabilitated in different places of the Garo Hills district and as well as for use as fire wood. The incalculable damage done to the forests of Garo Hills is inconceivable and this has obviously made tremendous impact on the environment of the Garo Hills. Although large scale deforestation, due to the practice of slash and burnt method of cultivation by the indigenous people of Garo Hills, it was aggravated by the refugee influx. Many of the immigrants were farmers and labourers, after rehabilitation they had to do something for livelihood. Some did not find any alternative means to sustain themselves except to cut firewood, bamboos and trees for sale to local people. This is an important cause of deforestation and even today some of them are still indulging in illicit and illegal felling of trees.

Impact on Demography and Economy of the Garo Hills District

Like other parts of the world, besides natural expansion, demography of Garo Hills District underwent considerable change due to immigration from as well as arrivals from other districts within the country. Geographically Garo Hills, District of Meghalaya, is located on the Indo-Bangladesh border. Most probably the huge number of immigrants from erstwhile East Pakistan boosted the existing number of population in Garo Hills districts during 1960's, which in turn aggravated the rapid growth of population in the state.

The census reports of the district have shown an increase in every decade since 1901, when the population was only 1,38,274. The density of population then was around 16 persons per square km. Even in 1951 there were only 2,42,075 persons in Garo Hills district. Within five decades (i.e. since 1901 to 1951) there was an increase of only 1,03,801. If we see 1971 census in which record has shows 4,06,615 people, where the number of increase can be seen as 1,64,540 within two decades (i.e. since 1951 to 1971) compared to the previous five decades.

From the Table 5.1 drastic change in percentage decadal variation in population can be seen within the period 1951-61. It was recorded as 26.91 per cent whereas in the previous decade it was only 08.28 per cent. This is on account of immigration. Since 1950's people from East Pakistan started to immigrate into the district of Garo Hills and other parts of Assam. During 1961-71 percentage increase in population in the district i.e. East and West Garo Hills is much higher than that of South Garo Hills district. It was probably because of displaced persons of East Pakistan who were rehabilitated within those 'district during 1960's.

Table 5.1: Variation in Population since 1901 to 2001 in Garo Hills Districts

Sl. No	District	Percentage decadal variation									
		1901-11	1911-21	1921-31	1931-41	1941-51	1951-61	1961-71	1971-81	1981-91	1991-01
1	2	3	4	5	6	7	8	9	10	11	12
1.	East Garo Hills	14.94	12.71	06.57	17.11	08.28	26.91	31.21	32.96	38.29	31.10
2.	West Garo Hills	14.94	12.71	06.57	17.11	08.28	26.91	37.98	23.04	31.06	27.98
3.	South Garo Hills	14.94	12.71	06.57	17.11	08.28	26.91	12.89	15.50	23.61	28.59

Source: Provisional Census Hand Book 2001, Meghalaya.

Density of population in Garo hills districts is increasing very rapidly in every decade but the per capita income is very low and most of the people are living under poverty line. The economic conditions of the people of Garo Hills has been adversely affected by the increased in population.

The countless number of refugees inundated the local population in Garo Hills. In order to earn money they resorted to sundry business activities at every available space, even on the busy footpath of the roadsides of towns like Tura, Williamnagar and Baghmara and in other pockets of Garo Hills. They used to purchase all kinds of food stuff from local people, and then resold them at exorbitant rates. In this way thousands of refugees from East Bengal brought-about unprecedented hardship and privations upon the bonafide children of the soil in Garo Hills district.

The untold number of workers and poorer sections, among the thousands of refugees from East Bengal, captured all sorts of existing labour jobs in Garo Hills, making labour exceedingly cheap. The poor daily wage-workers of the local area were rendered jobless; so much so that their family members were in extreme distress and were almost on the brink of starvation.

The immigration of East Pakistani people undoubtedly hampered the economic condition of Garo Hills. The districts are not economically developed. The natural resources are not fully utilised. In this situation the local Government had to release a huge amount of money for the relief and rehabilitation of the refugees.

In 1964 and 1971 mass influx the government had to face a sudden and an enormous problem of providing food, shelter, clothing and medicines to those people. Naturally Government had to postpone many of its development programmes and devote its time and energy to the relief and rehabilitation work at different places in the district.

The Government of India sanctioned Rs. 42,71,226 between 1964 and 1968 for relief and rehabilitation works under different schemes[1]. In an economically developing country like India this huge amount of money could have been used for some development work.

During the time of influx local people, living along the border, had to move to the interior places. They could not cultivate their land properly. On account of poor yield they could not pay their land revenue and house taxes etc. to District Council. The collection of tolls from the border markets were also disrupted causing loss to the District Council. Besides; normal work of the District Council was dislocated as all the members of the Executive Committee Officers and staff were engaged in relief work, though it was not possible to make correct assessment of the loss sustained by the District Council during those years, yet the amount of loss and expenditure incurred from the known resources was estimated to be Rs. 35,43,600.

Administrative expenditure incurred by District Council in connection with Relief and Rehabilitation works of 1964 refugees is as Table 5.2.

Table 5.2

Sl. No.	*Expenditure*	*Amount*
1.	Loss of revenue for random extraction of forest materials from USF, for camp construction and firewood etc, for refugees and the army. (1964-65 to 1969-70)	Rs. 16,07,000.00
2.	Loss of rent for occupation of District Council buildings at Tura-Chandmari and Rongram by the Government for relief works (1964-65 to 1969-70)	Rs. 1,46,000.00
3.	Expenditure in connection with the payment of T.A of the Members of the Executive Committee, and the Officers, cost of P.O.L and maintenance of vehicles used by them for relief works etc. (1964-65 to 1969-70)	Rs. 4,69,000.00
4.	Loss of revenue in respect of Hat Revenue, Fishery Revenue and Cattle Pounds etc. (1964-65 to 1969-70)	Rs. 12,46,400.00
5.	Expenditure incurred in connection with giving relief to people affected by the natural calamities.	Rs. 75,200.00
	Grand Total:	**Rs. 35,43,600.00**

Source: G.D.C's recorded regarding relief and rehabilitation works as on 18-5-77.

Table 5.3: Baghamara Range Baghmara 1964-65 to 1969-70

Sl. No	*Purpose for which utilised*	*Particulars*	*Quantity*	*Rate*	*Amount*
1.	Refugee Camp construction under 3rd batch at the following centre for which no forest revenue has been received.	Jungle wood poles of 30 to 45cm 200 × 24	48,000	@30p	14,400
	1. Baghmara Centre 350 sheds 2. Sibbari centre 450 sheds	Jati bamboos 200 × 20nos	40,000 nos	@ 10/-per 100 nos	4,000
	3. Dumnikura Centre 300 sheds	Tarai bamboos 2000 × 800 nos	16,00,000 nos	@ 4/- per 100 nos	64,000
	4. Mineng Centre 350 sheds 5. Dimapara Centre 300 sheds	Thatch grasses 2000 × 800 nos	16,00,000	@ 4/- per'000 nos	64,000
	6. Machangpani Centre 250 sheds				
	Total				**88,800**
2.	*Fire wood consumption by Refugees at the following centres.*				
	1. Moheskola Centre	20,000 person	36,00,000	@ 12p per bundle	4,32,000
	2. Mahadeo Centre	15,000 person			
	3. Rongara Centre	20,000 person			
	4. Oaobari Centre	10,000 person			
	5. Baghmara Centre	40,000 person			
	6. Sibbari Centre	20,000 person			
	7. Dumnikura Centre	15,000 person			
	8. Mineng Centre	10,000 person			
	9. Dimapara Centre	20,000 person			
	10. Machangpani Centre	10.000 person			
	11. Maguapara Centre & Chanduboi Centre	10,000 person			
	12. Sesengpara Centre.	10,000 person 2,00,000 person			
	Divided by average of 5 family members = 40,000 family for 3 days = 40,000 × 30/3 = 10 = 4,00,00 bundles for 9 month i.e. April/71 to Dectember/72 = 36,00,000 bundles				
3.	Fire wood sold by refugees approximate 1000 sellers at each centre for 12 centres = 12,000 × 30 days = 3,60, 000 bundles in a month × 9 months = 32,40,000 bundles		32,40,000 bundles	@ 12p per bundle	3,88,800
	Grant Total				**9.09.600**

Table 5.4: Mahendraganj Range

Sl. No	Purpose for which utilised	Particular	Quantity	Rate	Amount
1.	Fire wood consumption by the refugees at the following center . Idoba Centre . Ampati Centre . Patizora Centre . Kalaipara Centre . Purakhasia Centre . Chongnapara Centre . Halchati Centre . Noksi Centre . Dalamgre Centre of the population 22,600 families 1 load fire wood for each family for 3 days = 22600×30×9 / 3 for 9 months i.e. from April/71 to December/71	Fire wood	2034000 loads	@ 12p each	2,44,080
2.	Fire wood sold by refugees approximate 1000 sellers at each centre, 9 centre 900×30 days =2,70,000× 9 months	Fire wood	24,30,00	@ 12p each	2,91,600
	Grant Total				**Rs. 5,35,680**

Due to immigration there was a reduction in forest area. The farmers and labourers who migrated from East Pakistan cleared the forest for agriculture, camp construction and fire wood which is an important cause of deforestation. In 1971, thousands of East Pakistani people took to collection of firewood as their livelihood. Almost 2,00,000 persons from different centres of Baghamara range, using firewood for their domestic purposes, and around 12,000 families' directly engages themselves in collection of firewood from forest for their livelihood. From different centres of Mahendraganj 22,600 families are consuming fire word for cooking purpose and 9,000 sellers are depending upon forests for their livelihood. In term of money value it would come around Rs. 14,45,280 (Rupees fourteen lakh five thousand two hundred and eighty) only. These unscientific cutting of forest for agriculture, housing, domestic fuel etc caused tremendous impact on ecological balances in general and economy in particular.

Table 5.5: Statement of Financial Implication for Posting of Police Personal for Relief Camps in Garo Hills

1.	Total pay and allowance of 25 S.Is, 50 AS.Is, 200 constables (to be posted 1-S.I, 2-ASI & 8 constables each for 25 camps	7,10,400/-
2.	Total pay and allowance for 25 S.BS.Is, 25 S.BA.S.Is, 25 constables (to be posted 1-S.B.S.I, 2-S.BASI & 2 Constables each for 25 camps)	2,96, 550/-
3.	Dy. S.P (one)	5,460/-
4.	UB. Inspector of Police (5)	35,400/-
5.	10 drivers for 8 jeeps	23,880/-
6.	5 handymen	10,740/-
7.	10 drivers for 10 pickups	23,880/-
8.	10 handymen for 10 pickups	21,480/-
9.	one mechanic	2,521/-
10.	2UDAs	7,680/-
11.	6 LDAs	15,120/-
12.	1 Accountant	3.840/-
13.	1 Typist	2,520/-
14.	Daftry one	1,920/-
15.	2 UBSIs for reserve office	8,280/-
16.	2 ASIs for reserve office	5,760/-
17.	2 constable	4,320/-
18.	6 cooks	11,160/-
19.	6 water carriers	11,160/-
20.	6 sweepers	11,160/-
	Grand Total	**Rs. 19,32,730/-**

Others	
10 Jeeps @ 25,000/- each	2,50,000/-
10 Pickups @ 40,000/- each	4,00,000/-
2 Nos. typewriters	4,000/-
MMV	1,50,000/-
NCC	25,0007-
Cost of medicine	5,000/-
Clothing	1,00, 000/-
Ration	2,00, 000/-
T.A. of officers	4,000/-
TA. of Asst.	1,50,000/-
Telephone connection	3, 000/-
ONC	50,000/-
Organization works (Accommodation of office Asst. and Reserve staff Tura)	2,26,200/-
Total	35,00, 000/-

The Table 5.6 shows that the Government has spent a huge amount of money for relief works. It is also one of the factors which retards the country, rapid growth and development.

With the influx of Bangladeshi people some ancillary economic problems was faced by the Government such as:

(i) Education, health and sanitation.
(ii) Unemployment problem, both for the educated and the uneducated persons.
(iii) Reduction in per capita income of the people of Garo Hills district.
(iv) Low savings and low rate of capital formation.

Positive Impacts

Although the immigration of the East Pakistan people did

harm to the backward economy of Meghalaya, yet there were some positive contributions for the reconstruction of the existing economic system.

1. The Bangladeshi immigrants were generally labour oriented. They are generally skilled and trained labour in house construction (especially mud house), cane and bamboo works, tailoring, hair cutting, carpentry, leather works, etc. In order to under take their business they recruited indigenous youths as helpers. This created opportunities for the local youth to get training for their self-employment.
2. Since many of them were farmers, agricultural production has gone up considerably in Garo Hills district after the rehabilitation of the displaced persons in different parts of the district.
   - (i) More areas were brought under rice cultivation
   - (ii) Horticulture products went up
   - (iii) Animal husbandly, live stock, tanning, fishery, piggery, poultry farming and food processing etc. increased considerably and the economy of Garo Hills got a new dimension.
3. It increased the man power for the construction of roads and bridges and construction of buildings as well as in agriculture. Whereas local people are generally reluctant to perform this type of labour even though they were paid daily wages by the contractors. Transport and communication system is an important life-line of an economy. With the arrival of the refugees in Garo Hills transport and communication system considerably developed in order to transport goods from one place to another,

consequently the rural economy under went an improvement.

References

1. Kar, P.C., *Glimpses of the Garos*, Published by Das S.K. Hawakhana Tura, 1st Ed. 1982, p. 55.
2. *Ibid.*, p. 255.
3. Kar, P.C., *Glimpses of the Garos*, p. 280. And Marak Grohonsing A.: *Meghalaya stateko Maikai Man-aha*, p. 84.
4. Kar, P.C., *Glimpses of the Garos*, pp. 279-80.
5. *Ibid.*, pp. 225-56.
6. Vide Dewansing's complaint letter to Deputy Commissioner, Garo Hills Tura. Dated Baghmara the 3rd June, 1971.
7. *See* D.S. Rongmuthu's complaint letter, dated Baghmara the 3rd June, 1971.
8. Vide Short memorandum of the Garo Hills District Council-Date 18-5-77.

Appendix I

Mr. B.M. Rechil immigrated from Haluaghat of former East Pakistan in 1964. He is probably fifty eight years old. During the time of his entry to Garo Hills he was around 21 years old. He crossed the border during night in the month of July, 1964. His parents came ahead with other people in the month of February. He stayed back there till his B.A. final examination was over.

He studied upto class VIII in Oxford Mission at Haluaghat and upto class X in Biroi Daku's High School. He did his graduation from Brojomohan College, which was in the District of Baraisal and was affiliated to Dhaka University.

He told the authorities in Garo Hills that his parents were at Mineng Camp; before his arrival his parents were shifted to Matia camp of Goalpara District. One of his brothers did not come with them as he went to Gojarikura as a son-in-law. After crossing the border he stayed at Dalu for few days then shifted to Matia Camp in search of his parents.

Some of his relatives were living at Gasuapara and Ruga villages of Garo Hills district. Before they migrated to India his mother used to come to Megaram Marak of Ruga off and on.

He observed that during the time of his migration into India, particularly, in Garo Hills district, getting a job was not very difficult for a graduate. In Matia Camp he was given the job of Lower Division Assistant. Mr. Lawrence Ingty, who was deputed as O.S.D. to Matia camp, gave him that job. After six months he was given the job of an Accountant.

In 1965 he did his LL.B. in Shillong. From 1967 to 1972 he served as an Auditor in the Office of the Accountant General. Later he served as Law Officer in the Government of Meghalaya. He passed Meghalaya Civil Service in 1975. He was nominated to the Indian Administrative Service and served as Deputy Commissioner at Baghmara, headquarters of South Garo Hills District till his retirement on 30th November, 2001.

Mr. Bikas Rechil and his parents were rehabilitated at Govardhan in the District of Nawgong of Assam, under 'Khas Land' scheme and reclaimed land with homestead around 7 or 8 bighas were given to each family.

While they were at Matia Camp its condition was good, a hospital was established there. Everyday there were illness and death in the camp. Many of them were suffering from diarrhoea, Malaria and water borne diseases (like gastro-enteritis). In Matia camp there were around 60,000 refugees. Communities in the camp were A-chiks, Koches, Hajongs and Dalus. Among them largest number was the Garo Community. Bengalis were taken to the Boko camp. Sometime Public leaders also came to visit their camp. The government as well as the N.G.O's gave them rations, like rice, dal, mustard oil and other items. Ration card was issued to them after getting their names registered. For those who had migrated before 1971 citizenship certificate was given by the Government of India. Only in the year 1971 and onwards issuing of citizenship certificate was discontinued by the government of India. He took his citizenship certificate from the Deputy Commissioner of Goalpara district.

In East Pakistan it is difficult for the minority communities, though they might be highly educated, to get government jobs. Working in N.G.O's like World Vision and in the Mission are the only job openings for them. In India the immigrants have better job opportunities and security.

His wife worked as a staff nurse in Tura Christian Hospital, Tura and migrated from Bonopara in the same year as Bikas Marak Rechil. His father in-law worked at Mission Hospital at Tura (now Tura Christian Hospital).

He narrated the causes of the mass exodus in 1964: after the partition the Muslims of East Bengal began to repress the minorities. During 1960s this situation turned for the worse. They ill treated communities like Garos, Hajongs, Koches, Banais, Dalus and Bengalis etc. Most of the time victims were women and girls. Their movable and non-movable properties were looted, robbed and houses were set on fire by the Muslims. He himself was one of the persons, who rushed to the spot to help while dacoity was taking place in the houses of the Dalus of Gusbell village in East Pakistan. If they opposed such antisocial elements they were sometimes killed and assaulted. If they moved for prosecution in the court of justice or reported the matter to the police their appeals were not heard. He observed that these were the results of driving out of Muslims from Bihar. According to him there were many Muslim refugees from Bihar in the village nearby. In Mymensing alone there were around 40,000 Muslim refugees of Bihar. They were brought during the night into the (places) lands and homesteads abandoned by the minorities.

30-12-2001 **Mr. Bikas Marak Rechil**
Tura Tetengkol, Tura.

Appendix II

Land Meassurement

Unit of Area

120 ft. × 120 ft.	= 14400 sq. ft. in 1 bigha.
54 ft. × 54 ft.	= 2880 sq. ft. in 1 Kata.
12 ft. × 12 ft.	= 144 sq. ft. in 1 Lesa.
20 Lesa	= 1 Kata
5 Kata	= 1 Bigha.
100 Lesa	= 1 Bigha.
4840 sq. Yards in 1 Acre.	
About 2½ Acre	= 1 Hectare.
100 m × 100 m	= 10,000 sq.m. in Hectare.
B -K -L	
6 1 5	= 1 Hectare.
40 m × 40 m	= 1600 sq.m. in 1 Bigha.
	320 sq.m. in 1 Kata.
4m × 4m	= 16 sq.m. in 1 Lesa.

Appendix III

Khasi and Jaintia Hills of Meghalaya. Number of persons in camp since 26-03-1971 upto 06-06-1971.1.

	Name of Camps	*No. of Persons in Camp*
A. Dawki Sector		
1.	Amlarem	5530
2.	Madan Lyngtad	8124
3.	Madan Baitah	5442
4.	Pongtung	1466
5.	Amtronge	4319
6.	Reception Centre Dawki and Lynkhat	33
B. Shella Sector		
7.	Shella	7819
8.	Ichamati	5709
9.	Reception Centre Bholaganj and Tyllab	2177
10.	Mailam	16702
11.	Balat	4005
C. Gomaghat Sector		
12.	Monai	5918
13.	Reception Centre Gomaghat & Moheskola	2759
	Total	**79,394**

Appendix IV

The Awami League's six-points programme mentioned below represents a rational solution to the problem of regional injustice.

1. A federal parliamentary system of Government, elected on adult franchise.
2. The Federal Government to deal only with defence and foreign affairs.
3. Either two Separate Currencies for the two wings or one common currency, with Constitutional Safe guards against the flight of Capital from East to West Pakistan.
4. Neither power of taxation nor revenue collection shall vest in the Centre, these shall be the exclusive preserves of Ac federating units.
5. Foreign Exchange transaction and earnings shall be under the control of the federating Units; and
6. A Militia or Para-military force shall be set up in East Pakistan.

Bibliography

Primary Sources

(A) Persons Interviewed

1. Bikash Marak Rechil, Tura Te-tengkol, Tura, West Garo Hills, on 30-12-2001.
2. Crunden S. Sangma, Upper Chandmary, Tura West Garo Hills, on 29-12-2001.
3. Amarendra Simsang Sangma, Bonepa A-tila, Tura, on 29-12-2001.
4. Mihir. N. Sangma, Proper Chandmary, Tura, on 29-12-2001.
5. Mitra N. Sangma, Nehru A-ding, Tura on 29-12-2001.
6. Dinesh Chandra Sangma, Tura Matchakol, Tura on 30-12-2001.
7. Ananta Sangma, Araimlie, New Tura, on 30-12-2001.
8. Bilsing Ch. Marak, Danakgre, West Garo Hills, on 19-01-2002.
9. Monoronjon Sangma, Gimegre, West Garo Hills, on 27-01-2002.
10. Horesh Mankin Sangma and his wife Smt. Bosilla Dajel Marak, Rongkongre, P.O. Rongmatchok, West Garo Hills on 28-01-2002.
11. Noho Rechil Marak and his wife Smt. Beromka Mankin Sangma, Rongkongre, West Garo Hills, on 28-01-2002.
12. Jotindra Marak, Batabari Chirakawa West Garo Hills, on 29-01-2002.

13. Admiral Marak, Batabari Chirakawa, West Garo Hills, on 29-01-2002.
14. Sotindra Chisim, Singwilgre, West Garo Hills, on 29-01-2002.
15. Dinesh Rema, Chokchokia, West Garo Hflls, on 29-01-2002.
16. Father Mani K.M. St. John Mary Vianney Mission, Chokchokia, on 29-01-2002.
17. Wilson Rechil, Balaehanda, West Garo Hills, on 29-01-2002.
18. Mina Kumar Rechil, WilUampiir (Nidanpur), West Garo Hills, on 30-01-2002.
19. Stanlee Sangma, Demdemma, West Garo Hills, on 30-01-2002.
20. Kolindro M. Marak, Gimejora (Demdemma), West Garo Hills, on 03-02-2002.
21. Albinstone M. Sangma, Mondol Barrack, Tura Hawakhana, Tura on 04-03-2003.
22. Grohonsing A, Marak, Hawakhana Tura on, 09-02-2002,
23. Bibash D. Sangma and Shri. Wasington Marak, in Garo Hills District Council Office, Tura, on 05-03-2002.
24. Roosevelt Ch. Marak, Bonepa A-tilla, Tura, on 08-03-2002.
25. Tapon Marak, Hawakhana Council Quarter, Tura on 09-02-2002.
26. Janseng N. Marak, Ku-simkolgre, East Garo Hills, Williamnagar, on 10-03-2002.
27. Robin Rema, Tura, Hawakhana, (Near Circuit House) Tura on 11-05-2003.

(B) Files and Bundles

(i) Files available at D.C's Office, West Garo Hills, Tura.

(a) File No. GRRO 1/64/...... Accommodation of Refugees.

(b) File No. GRRO 3/64/......Health and Sanitation.
(c) File No. GRRO 7/64/....... Statistical on Refugees.
(d) File No. GRRO 10/64/...... Miscellaneous.
(e) File No. GRRO 14/64/...... Construction of Shed Collection of Materials for Camps.
(f) File No. GRRO 15/64/..... Education facilities to the Refugee Students.
(g) File No. GRRO 16/64/..... Resettlement of Refugee, release from Camps.
(h) File No. GRRO 28/64/..... W.T. Message of daily registration.

(ii) Different File Nos. of /RRG/71 and TRN/71 available at D.C.'s Office, West Garo Hills Tura.
(iii) Files available at Garo Hills Autonomous District Council Office, Land Revenue Branch, West Garo Hills, Tura.

(C) Published Documents

Shira Lindrid D., Dewansing PvOngmuthu, (Agrango Ekilgipa Sa-atalo Gisikgipa/Gisik Mafgrik), D.V.S. Publishers, Guahati, 1999.

Kar P.C., *Glimpses of the Garos* Published by Das. S.K., Tura First Ed. 1982.

Marak G.A., Meghalaya State-ko maikai Man-aha, Tura, 1993.

(D) Unpublished Document

(a) *The Bangladesh and the Background* by Grohonsing A. Marak, Tura.
(b) Memoranda Submitted by Dewansing Rongmuthu Baghmara 3rd June 1971.

Secondary Sources

Burling R., Rengsanggre, Second Ed. 1997. *Tura Book Rom, Tura.*

Malayalam Manorama, *Manorama Year Book 2002*, 37th Edition.

Provisional Census Hand Book 2001, Meghalaya

Sangma Samson K. (1979) "*Garo Geography of Assam, Meghalaya India and Pakistan in Outline*".

Index

A

All Party Hills Leaders' Conference 89
Ampati Camps 11, 34
anti-Pakistani 50
Arbella range 12
Armed Police camps 51
Assam 11, 13, 16, 37, 40, 46, 50, 72, 81, 94
Assam Rifles 38
Assistant Relief and Rehabilitation Officer 8
Australian Baptist Mission 49
Autonomy for East Bengal 55
Awami Leader 58
Awami League 54–55, 57, 60, 110

B

Balpakram 14
Bangladesh 9, 12, 14, 19–20, 37, 44
Bangladesh Liberation 21, 25, 27, 34, 81
Bangladesh Refugees 25, 28
Bhutto, Z.A. 54, 55
Bihar 42
Bodo Speaking Groups 14
Brahmaputra 13–14

C

Central Reseve Police Force (CRPF) 29
Chandabhoi 35
China 14
Christian Agency for Social Action (CASA) 34
Citizenship Act 73
Civil Disobedience Movement 56
Communist Party of India (CPI) 89
Community Development Block 43
Conservation Scheme 69–70
Constitution of India 87
Cooch Behar 13

D

Dadengre sub-division 11
Dalu Relief Camp 23
Destruction of a Muslims Shrine 42

Dewani of Bengal 15
Dimapara 33
Diversionary Measures 53

E

East Pakistan 9
East Pakistan Riffles 44–45, 48

F

Forcible Conversions 43, 51
Foreigner Registration 37
Foreigners Registration Act 81

G

Gandhi, Indira 9
Ganol Camp 21, 25
Garo Baptist Convention 33
Garo Christian 23
Garo Community 48
Garo Hills 9, 11–16, 19–20, 34, 40–41, 43–44, 47, 50, 60, 64–65, 72, 81
  Economic Condition of 96
  Density of Population in 95
Garo Hills Autonomous District Council 38
Garo Hills District 20, 25, 65–67, 71–73, 87–88
Garo Migrant Families 71
Garo National Council (GNC), 88
Garo Refugees 25, 65
Garo Welfare Organisation 49
Goalpara 13
Government of India Act 49
Gram Sevak 43

H

Habraghat Pargana 13
Himalaya 14
Hwang-Ho 14

I

Illicit and Illegal felling of Trees 93
Indian National Congress 88, 90
Indian Red Cross Society 32
Indo-Pakistan Boundary Tribunal 51
Influx Effect of the 90

K

Khan, Ayub 48, 53
Khan, General Yahya 53, 57, 58
Khan, Major Zia 59
Khan, Tikka 60
Khan, Yahya 54, 57
Khan, Zia 59
Khas Land Scheme 67, 73, 105

L

Land Reclamation 10
Liberation Army of Bangladesh 59
Lido-Pakistan Border Belt 50
London 60
Looting 41

M

Marak, Ghoronsing A. 42, 52, 65, 90
Marak, Tapan 38
Martial Law 53, 57, 59
Matia Camp 25, 104–05
Meghalaya 9, 11–12, 20, 30, 34, 37–38, 40, 43, 50, 73, 81
Mineng Camp 32, 104
Minority Communities 41
Mizoram 20, 40, 43
Mymensing District 16, 19–20, 43, 49

N

NGOs 106
National Assembly 53, 54
Nehru, Jawaharlal 51
Nengminja, Togan 16
Non-cooperation Movement 60
North Goalpara Garo Baptist Union 33
North Mymensing District 50

P

Pakistan Peoples Party 54
Partition Committee 49–50
Peoples Republic of Bangladesh 58
Political Parties Act 53

R

R.R Camps 30
Ramakrishna Mission 33–35
Rechil, B.M. 38, 42, 104, 105
Refugee Camps 20–21
Registration Card 81
Rehabilitation Centre of Migrant Families 75
Rehabilitation Measures 72, 97
Rehman, Sheikh Mujibur 54, 55, 56, 57, 58, 60, 61
Relief and Rehabilitation Department 21
Religious Intolerance 48
Resubelpara Subdivision 11
Ringge River 12
Rioting and Robbery 41
Rongai Valley Project 12
Rongmuthu, Dewanshing S. 32, 49, 91
Rongnabok Relief Camps 38
Rongram Relief Camp 23

S

Sangma, Amarendra Simsang 43
Sangma, Ananta 44, 52
Sangma, Binoy Bhusan 50
Sangma, Dinesh Chandra 44
Sangma, Emonsing M. 90
Sangma, Mitra. N. 32
Sangma, Mononronjon 45
Sangma, W.A. 15, 44, 64, 65, 87, 88, 90
Scott, David 15
Shifting of the Refugees 10
Simsang river 16
Singh, J.P. 29
Six-point Programme 56, 110
Small Trader Scheme 71

Soil Conservation Department 65
Surmah Valley 12
Swadhin Bangladesh Kendra 59
Sylhet Districts 52

T

Tibet 14
Tibeto-Burman race 14
Tikrikifla Area 72
Tin Hata Mission 43
Tripura 20, 40, 43
Tura Christian Hospital 106

U

Under State Forest (USF) 93
Union Christian College 38

V

Voluntary Organizations 36

W

Waldheim, Kurt 51
Weekly Markets 15
West Bengal 38, 40
White, V.J. 49, 50
Wiffiamson, W.J. 16

Y

Yang-Tse-Kiang 14

Z

Zamindar 15–16